The Self-Writing Universe

The Self-Writing Universe

For the Eternally Curious

Phil Scanlan

www.philscanlan.net

iUniverse, Inc.
New York Lincoln Shanghai

The Self-Writing Universe
For the Eternally Curious

iUniverse, Inc.

For information address:
iUniverse, Inc.
2021 Pine Lake Road, Suite 100
Lincoln, NE 68512
www.iuniverse.com

ISBN: 0-595-31777-4

Printed in the United States of America

In studied dedication to the twisting, turning, rolling of the mighty, mighty, mighty—Very Fine Theme.

CONTENT

ACKNOWLEDGEMENTS

This book could not have been written without the patient understanding of my editor and father, Gerald Scanlan.

INTRODUCTION

The nothingness "before" the creation of the universe is the most complete void that we can imagine—no space, time, or matter existed. It is a world without place, without duration or eternity, without number—it is what mathematicians call "the empty set." Yet this unthinkable void converts itself into the plenum of existence—a necessary consequence of physical laws. Where are these laws written into the void? What "tells" the void that it is pregnant with a possible universe? It would seem that even the void is subject to law, a logic that exists prior to space and time.

Heinz Pagels, *Perfect Symmetry*, 1985

The difference between words and knowledge can be subtle. Most of us have the ability to spout off words, but the most talkative among us are not necessarily the most knowledgeable. Conversely, the person that doesn't talk much sometimes just doesn't have anything to say. Even so, knowledge *must* be conveyed with words (or more generically *symbols*) for it to be understandable. So then, what's the intrinsic difference between spouting off words and conveying knowledge?

I believe the difference between words and knowledge has to do with conveying *process*, the way things work as only hinted at by the words. When the process of how something works can be effectively conveyed, we have knowledge.

This book considers the most confounding puzzle we can ask ourselves— *how and why is there anything at all instead of simply nothingness?* This is the puzzle of existence.

I suggest that the puzzle of existence can be solved by viewing it as though it were a computer script that managed to write itself: a script that was written because it had to be written, naturally. A computer script is a list of commands that can be executed on a computer without user interaction. Network administrators use scripts all the time to automate various tasks in a networked environment. Such scripts do not write themselves, however, so I'm obviously using the idea of a self-writing computer script as an analogy to help us better understand how the universe could have self-started. As of now, such a suggestion is merely a string of spouted off words. What we're looking for is the process behind the words.

In this book, our singular goal is to find the most logically correct and consistent way of viewing the puzzle of existence so that we can understand its process. We will be viewing the puzzle as though it were a procedurally based computer script—meaning that one thing happens after another in a series of events with all resulting behavior explainable by a line or more of executable code (note: combinations of code may still occasionally result in unexplainable errors!). In short, we will be looking at the puzzle of existence as though it were the sort of thing that can be solved.

By this way of thinking, the fact that there's existence and not non-existence is merely due to some line (or more) of executable code that makes existence inevitable. So, we'll be considering what that code must be like. We'll be asking how that code got there and how it avoids the fallacy of explaining existence by first assuming an existing thing (in this case, a line of executable code!). These are age-old questions and conundrums. So too are these the eternal questions that we as humans are privileged to be capable of asking.

It is our responsibility as thinking entities living in this cosmos to ask ourselves the eternal question: how and why is there anything at all instead of simply nothingness? It is our joy to uncover the process that explains how such a thing works. There is no greater intellectual puzzle. There is no greater intellectual reward.

In exchange for your time and concentration, I promise to convey a deep insight into what I believe to be the mechanics of existence. I believe we are fortunate to have this opportunity to take this journey together, and I am honored to be your guide. Beware there is a lot of intellectual terrain for us to navigate in order to provide the appropriate context. I promise to guide you through it with as few scrapes and bruises as possible.

But realize that this book is a trailblazer. You won't find any other book out there that tackles the puzzle of existence in as direct and focused a manner as this one. When you blaze your own trail, you're bound to take a few missteps. Most people simply assume that the puzzle of existence is unanswerable: incomprehensible. Trailblazing can be difficult. Sideline critics might harp on the missteps and ignore the big picture. Understand that the one or two missteps we'll undoubtedly take in this book will be overshadowed by the attainment of our ultimate goal. I believe that at the end of our journey the puzzle of existence will seem a much more understandable beast than it did at the beginning. We will not be denied.

Whether we actually solve the puzzle of existence here or not will remain, of course, empirically unanswerable. The very nature of this puzzle is that it's empirically untestable. Just the same, we'll take a stab at making the previously incomprehensible understandable. We'll touch the eternal, if only for a moment, by immersing ourselves in the process of creation…Curious for more?

The Eternal Quest

Humanity has long sought to solve the riddle of the universe's creation. Our earliest ancestors, once they attained a spark of intelligence, no doubt looked at the heavens in awe and wonderment yet without having a clue as to what it all meant and how it came about. Millenniums have passed and how much more do we really know about creation than our prehistoric ancestors? Having thought about this phenomenon for a fair number of years now, I have come to the conclusion that the answer is—not much.

I do not claim to be a scientist nor a professional philosopher. At the risk of being branded a non-expert, my perspective is unabashedly that of a network administrator and computer expert. I believe this perspective provides me with the background from which to develop a unique insight. After all, we're dealing with an empirically unanswerable puzzle—why and how is there anything at all instead of simply nothingness? Science alone, by definition, will never be able to solve this puzzle (it's empirically unanswerable!), and philosophy can only—well, your guess is as good as mine.

I am convinced that the puzzle of existence needs new insight. In theory, such an insight should spring from the realm of philosophy. Professional philosophers have however been woefully timid in attempting to unravel the puzzle of existence. Since no other field has stepped up to the plate, *why not* the computer networking field? *Why not* view the puzzle as though it were a computer script that managed to write itself and see what happens?

My dilemma has always been that I am dissatisfied with the God or Chance theories that have been offered as the answer to how the universe was created. I am against neither God nor Chance, but I believe such answers merely beg the question. After all, in each case an existing thing is being used to explain existence—how convenient! While my alternative theory may be as empirically unverifiable as the others, I submit it offers an insight into how the puzzle could have solved itself, naturally. With this in mind, I offer this project for what it is worth, requesting only that the reader retain an open mind. Basically, what I'm

suggesting is that I want the reader to be consciously open to challenging any pre-conceived opinions and beliefs. My conclusion that the universe was created by a default process—a self-writing Script—may stimulate and/or depress the reader, but in actuality the conclusion reached is probably a very close approximation of how it all began. And, more fundamentally, I believe my theory represents a logi-cally consistent way of viewing and untangling a classic conundrum.

The theory I present in *The Self-Writing Universe* has been influenced by my experience in the field of network computing. Consequently, you'll find that I use the computer analogy quite extensively in this book. Remember when con-sidering this analogy that we are talking about a subject matter that is impossi-ble to perform scientific experiments on. Nevertheless, the universe's behavior really does seem to be procedurally-based, i.e., operating to a significant extent *like* a computer executing commands from a script. If true, the universe might well have started up much like a computer would start up if it had a self-writing program.

Please note that this book avoids the ubiquitous Chapters in favor of Bytes. Computers use binary numbers (1's and Ø's). The word **bit** is a shortening of the words "Binary digIT." Bits are rarely seen alone in computers. They are almost always bundled together into 8-bit collections, and these collections are called **bytes:**

1 bit	= basic unit of measurement
1 byte	= 8 bits
1 kilobyte (kb)	= 1024 bytes
1 megabyte (mb)	= 1,048,576 bytes
1 gigabyte (gb)	= 1,073,741,824 bytes

Due to this basic unit of measurement in the world of computers, I use **BYTE** in this book to signify Chapter.

Note: Not everyone is a professional philosopher, nor is everyone a profes-sional scientist. Nor *should* everyone be either one or the other; that would make for a boring world. While I have great respect for most professional philosophers and scientists I believe that their solutions to the great puzzle have thus far been inadequate. As mentioned, my area of expertise happens to be with computers; my particular niche being in the area of network security and desktop administration. This vantage point has allowed me to see classical conundrums anew and with a unique insight.

BYTE ONE:

THE HUMAN FACTOR

http://www.philscanlan.net/

© 2004 by Phil V. Scanlan

Welcome: We Are Here

How wonderful that we have met with paradox. Now we have some hope of making progress.

—Niels Bohr

This book covers a lot of science as interpreted and discussed by scientists in scholarly books and essays. This book, however, is not a work of science. Even so, science is not meaningful without interpretation. The funny thing though about interpretations, and people in general, is that they're messy. Don't get me wrong, we still have science—it's just not some pristine absolute—much is subjective.

The idea that scientific facts can even exist without a subjective interpretive spin, or that these spins are not actively argued for and against by scientists to persuade other scientists (along with laypeople) is unrealistic. There is almost nothing scientifically set in stone. In science, a theory is really only as good as the last experiment that supports it. Because the world is generally stable and follows obvious patterns and cycles, we tend to harden the experimentally supported theories into absolutes. That's psychology, and has nothing to do with the actual method of science.

Scientific laws are not independent truths. They are context-dependent regularities. Consider Newtonian gravity which has features that match our universe nicely, such as elliptical orbits. Consider also Relativity theory. It has features that Newton's system lacks. What we have to confront is the very real likelihood that our universe probably relies on neither to go about its business; Newton's and Einstein's theories are models, not ultimate truths. Good models, brilliant models, but who today can seriously believe that these laws are absolute?

The grade-school model of scientific progress suggests that humans began in superstitious ignorance and have since been progressing steadily closer toward final truth. This overly-simplistic, ultra-linear model has long been discredited. We have learned instead that science is not some ultra-rational pursuit of objective information, devoid of any subjective agendas. Science is rather a creative human activity; its leading geniuses often seeming to be more like artists than scientists.

We are now familiar with how difficult it is for a change in scientific theory to occur. New evidence, new discoveries are not enough to force a change from the inertia of the prevalent scientific model. A change in theory depends not only on new discoveries and findings, but also on the creative imagination of the advocate and his or her ability to persuade and influence contemporary social and political forces inside the scientific community. The singular aspect that continues to make science special, however, is that it's still the most objective and intellectually accepted method by which to study and understand how the world works.

Make no mistake, agendas and interpretations are a constant in any form of thought, including science. And this book has its own agenda, its own interpretation that will be packaged in as persuasive a manner as possible by an imperfect author using the findings of an imperfect science. Such agendas and interpretations represent unavoidable baggage that any reader is forced to filter through when reading an intellectual thesis. As if this interpretational baggage wasn't enough, we have other cognitive limitations that are even more difficult for us to deal with. Truth be told, we are not omniscient. There is much we don't know.

What makes us believe we can overcome our cognitive limitations to solve something as abstract as the puzzle of existence? More generally, even if we were lucky enough to stumble across The Answer, what makes us believe we'd be smart enough to realize it? The remainder of this BYTE is dedicated to the answering of these questions.

Nonsense and Superstition

For those of you who are serious advocates of something or other, I encourage you to give this a try—force yourself to assume the exact opposite position of that which you are passionate, no matter how absurd it may seem. Doing so provides a great sense of freedom, much like a weight being lifted from off your back. It's kind of like re-discovering your innocence; rediscovering that the world is somewhat crazy-ass and borderline incoherent.

After all, there's always the possibility, on some deeply disturbing level, that your beliefs really *are* wrong. Accordingly, it's important, I feel, to keep our wits about things and to keep active a lively sense for the irrational. To that end, I have included this section as it gently queries (self-referentially) whether or not the very theory I'm proposing in answer of the greatest of all puzzles is simply gibberish. Hence, before this discussion can go further we'll need to familiarize ourselves with the nature of nonsense so that we can spot it when it's before us.

Carl Sagan, the late scientist, gave a nice overview of some of the irrational things people are known to believe:

> Typical offerings of pseudoscience and superstition—this is merely a representative, not a comprehensive list—are astrology; the Bermuda Triangle; "Big Foot" and the Loch Ness monster; ghosts; the "evil eye"; multicolored halolike "auras" said to surround the heads of everyone (with colors personalized); extrasensory perception (ESP), such as telepathy, precognition, telekinesis, and "remote viewing" of distant places; the belief that 13 is an "unlucky" number (because of which many no-nonsense office buildings and hotels in America pass directly from the 12th to the 14th floors—why take chances?); bleeding statues; the conviction that carrying the severed foot of a rabbit around with you brings good luck; divining rods, dowsing, and water witching; "facilitated communication" in autism; the belief that razor blades stay sharper when kept inside small cardboard pyramids, and other tenets of "pyramidology"; phone calls (none of them collect) from the dead; the prophecies of Nostradamus; the alleged discovery that untrained flatworms can learn a task by eating the ground-up remains of other, better educated flatworms; the notion that more crimes are committed when the Moon is full; palmistry; numerology; polygraphy; comets, tea leaves, and "monstrous" births as harbingers of future events (plus the divinations fashionable in earlier epochs, accomplished by viewing entrails, smoke, the shapes of flames, shadows, and excrement; listening to gurgling stomachs; and even, for a brief period, examining tables of logarithms); "photography" of past events, such as the crucifixion of Jesus; a Russian elephant that speaks fluently; "sensitives" who, when carelessly blindfolded, read books with their fingertips; Edgar Cayce (who predicted that in the 1960s the "lost" continent of Atlantis would "rise") and other "prophets," sleeping and awake; diet quackery; out-of-body (e.g., near-death) experiences interpreted as real events in the external world; faith-healer fraud; Ouija boards; the emotional lives of geraniums, uncovered by intrepid use of a "lie detector"; water remembering what molecules used to be dissolved in it; telling character from facial features or

bumps on the head; the "hundredth monkey" confusion and other claims that whatever a small fraction of us wants to be true really is true; human beings spontaneously bursting into flame and being burned to a crisp; 3-cycle bio-rhythms; perpetual motion machines, promising unlimited supplies of energy (but all of which, for one reason or another, are withheld from close examination by skeptics); the systematically inept predictions of Jeane Dixon (who "predicted" a 1953 Soviet invasion of Iran and in 1965 that the USSR would beat the U.S. to put the first human on the Moon) and other professional "psychics"; the Jehovah's Witnesses' prediction that the world would end in 1917, and many similar prophecies; dianetics and Scientology; Carlos Castaneda and "sorcery"; claims of finding the remains of Noah's Ark; the "Amityville Horror" and other hauntings; and accounts of a small brontosaurus crashing through the rain forests of the Congo Republic in our time. (Sagan, 1996)

As lengthy a list as this is, I cannot believe that Sagan missed cloud-zapping. However this may be, Sagan's point was that these things are silly to believe in because either there's evidence against them, or because science has advanced enough to reject them on principle.

As regards the former, believers can often-times skirt around this, due to the type of belief that they have—i.e., one for which there's simply no evidence to be found for or against it. However, what these believers cannot skirt around is the more subtle claim that **if** their belief is clearly contrary to known physics, **then** the burden of proof is on their belief. Until there's evidence to support it, there's no reason to hold the belief (of course, you can always keep an open mind about things, but that's a far cry from holding an unsupportable belief).

People occasionally get confused with this, thinking that it's healthy to stoke the market-place of possibility. They might claim that until there's proper evidence to refute a given claim, it should be treated as potentially valid. This is misguided. While it's true that many things are not known *a priori* and that much trial and error and experience is needed before we can truly hope to understand them (for example, even the laws of physics were not known until *after* suitable experiments were performed), it doesn't therefore follow that all views are equally probable. All views might have correctly seemed of equal probability a thousand or so years ago, but that was long before progress in science pulled away many of the layers of obscurity from our world. Given our present scientific knowledge, there's no longer any excuse (save ignorance) to steadfastly believe in something that is completely opposite what the sciences tell us concerning how the world works. This is especially so given the fact that we now have a number of well-tested principles about how the world operates. In sum, an open mind is one thing, but science works—and since we reside on a type of world where science does in fact work, we should certainly respect that.

Too often, however, this is not heeded. In this regard, let's consider the principle called "Ockam's Razor" as attributed to William of Ockam, a Franciscan monk of the 13th century. He suggested that "entities should not be multiplied beyond their necessity." For instance, if a track of footprints is spotted during a hike that look suspiciously similar to human footprints, then why envision a host of fairies, gremlins, and angels, that could all be used in conjunction (somehow) to explain the exact same footprints, but in a very unnecessary sort of way?

Rarely, however, is such a principle as clear in practice as it appears in theory. In fact, Ockam's Razor does not always work quite in the way intended. Sometimes preconceptions and misplaced skepticism get in the way of clean, sharp slicing (by Razor, of course). An oft-cited case of this (by proponents of UFOs, ghosts, and many other things) is the French Academy's prolonged rejection of the reality of meteorites. It wasn't until 1803 that the French Academy of Sciences finally recognized meteorite falls as a scientific phenomenon. Prior to that, dozens of meteorites were thrown out of European museums, on the advice of the finest scientific opinion of the day. The scientists had concluded that the belief rocks could fall from the sky was a product of superstitious nonsense. Well, (some have argued) if such a mistake in reasoning could happen before, couldn't it happen again?

Yes, of course it could. But what kind of criterion is that? I could sprout wings and fly to the Moon. I could, I could. By default, you see, we are forced to limit (as best we can), the unlimited. Anything, in principle, could happen. But not all things do. And science, along with Ockam's Razor, is the best method we know of to understand how and why some things happen and other things don't.

The Woolly World

From woolly minds come woolly thoughts? If only it were that simple. Not all UFO enthusiasts, Mystics, and other such believers, are simple-minded or even obviously *incorrect*. Sometimes events in the world really are rather mysterious. We cannot assume by reason alone that there either are or are not visiting space aliens. The same applies to any supposed paranormal experience. There's nothing logically impossible about such phenomena. Accordingly, the way to solve the issue is through empirical evidence. What does the evidence

suggest? Is it sufficient enough to warrant the adoption of a particular hypothesis (for instance, "space aliens are visiting us")? If the evidence is inconclusive or flatly opposite the contention, then the adoption of the hypothesis is not warranted. That's because the burden of proof is on the hypothesis, not the other way around. Otherwise, we run into faulty conclusions. Let's visit, as way of illustration, our soon-to-be-beloved friend, the Ham Sandwich.

The Ham Sandwich

I contend that a magical Ham Sandwich exists and it visits me every night—in fact we have milk and cookies together. As proof, I point to two empty glasses with milk residue and two crumb-laden napkins. I have even filmed such a cookie-eating session on my camcorder. Of course, the Ham Sandwich doesn't show up on film as he's the Ham Sandwich (invisible to film), so that certainly can't count *against* my claim. In point of fact, the Ham Sandwich's milk and cookies are always consumed at the end of each visit.

Now let it be known that I'm an upstanding citizen. I pay my taxes and have a full-time job. I enjoy my privacy and my family life. I have nothing to gain by pulling any kind of stunt. In fact, I'm insulted at the very suggestion that this *might be* a stunt. This Ham Sandwich thing is a serious matter and it warrants scientific study. Indeed, I invite somebody, *anybody*, to help me explain this phenomenon.

The local news reports my story and it becomes well known, and then the mass media picks up on it and it quickly becomes an international sensation. Soon, other people report having had the same type of cookie-eating experience. Evidently they had been too embarrassed to report it earlier, but now they thought the time was right to come forward. Surprisingly, thousands end up having a variation of my original experience. All of these people are "honest and decent" and sincerely believe that what they say is true. At this point, would it not be prudent to claim "certainly so many honest and decent people couldn't be wrong? Yes. Something must be going on here." And so a faction of Ham Sandwich enthusiasts is born.

The point of all this is that without a *burden of proof*, any sort of nonsense—no matter how unsupported and absurd—must be considered acceptable. The Ham Sandwich analogy applies to UFOs, visions of Mary and Christ, big foots, ghosts and goblins, and most any other paranormal occurrence. Any one of these phenomena is possible, yet that by itself does not provide legitimacy. What's more, just because many people believe really really strongly in something does not equate to actual proof.

Let's say that a couple of years pass by. The fuss about eating cookies with the Ham Sandwich has mostly subsided (although there are still a few reported occurrences). For whatever reason I decide to admit that I made it all up. I thought it would be harmless and fun, but then it just kind of took off on me, and I couldn't back out. I explain in detail how I cleverly turned off the camcorder and simply ate the "Ham Sandwich's" milk and cookies myself once the camcorder stopped recording. My confession receives some press, but not much. The Ham Sandwich enthusiasts pay it no mind. They say my reprehensible behavior certainly can't explain the multitude of other sightings. And so the phenomenon endures and the believers continue to believe.

Ridiculous? Things don't happen like that? Well then, let's take a look at *crop circles*.

Crop Circles

This phenomenon originated in Great Britain and quickly spread throughout the world. "Crop circles" refers to the images impressed upon fields of wheat, oats, barley, and rapeseed (as seen in the movie *Signs*). The crop circles of the mid 1970s were simple circles, but by the late 1980s they had advanced enough to display complex geometrical figures the size of football fields.

At the time, almost everyone agreed that these crop circles could not have been a hoax: there were too many of them and on much too large of a scale. Any supposed pranksters would not have had enough hours in the night to pull off such a stunt. Also, there were rumored to be no footprints leading either toward or away from the crop circles. And, in any case, what possible motive could there be to create such a hoax?

The number of crop circles soon rose into the thousands—spreading into the United States, Canada, Bulgaria, Hungary, Japan, and the Netherlands. As the pictograms grew more and more complex, the argument for alien visitations seemed to strengthen. For how could simple man create such elegant and complex figures without being discovered?

But this wonderful fantasy was destroyed by reality. In 1991, Doug Bower and Dave Chorley revealed that they had been making crop circles for some fifteen years. They had originally dreamed it up due to their amusement over UFO reports and thought it might be fun to spoof the gullibles. At first, the crop circles took them only a few minutes work, but gradually the design and execution became more and more involved.

When their crop circles finally became noticed by the media—eventually becoming of interest to the brain-trust of UFOlogists—Bower and Chorley were delighted. How amusing for them when scientists and learned others announced that no mere human could have created such crop circles. How proud they must have been to see copycats appear in southern England and then elsewhere. A more successful prank is hard to imagine. By 1991, however, Bower and Chorley, both in their sixties, had lost the zeal for creating crop circles, and duly confessed. As it turned out, the media paid little attention to this—the story was reported and then dropped (apparently not having the imaginative flair of possible UFO visitations).

And the UFOlogists? A simple argument and their beliefs are maintained: "Well, just because some crop circles turned out to be hoaxes, it doesn't follow that all must have been hoaxes." True enough. But there's no evidence for anything other than a hoax! (Sagan, 1996, p.73-6)

Perhaps, then, the reader will agree that there is not much of a mystery to the phenomenon of crop circles. However, you may say to yourself, "there are many other mysteries that have nothing to do with crop circles." Well, that's probably true enough, but it does nevertheless provide a sober testimony to people's propensity to believe in abject nonsense.

Illusions

So, we're gullible enough to occasionally believe in abject nonsense. That's certainly an all-too-human limitation. Yet, so long as we stick to the scientific method we can seemingly avoid getting duped into believing most nonsensical things. Can we carry on with our lives now? Have we no more human limitations to consider?

But wait, there's more.

Consider illusions. Many illusions trick and confuse us. Each of us believes we have an intuitive "inside" understanding of the world, unlike anyone else, and that we are therefore generally right in our intuitions while others are generally not so right. Such a belief, of course, is a deep-level illusion. We see mirages in the distant road. We hear the ocean in seashells and see the moon as being bigger when nearer the Earth's horizon than when not. As the car next to us creeps slowly forward, we wonder for a second if our car might be mistakenly in reverse. In time's past, we even saw canals on Mars. We're constantly fooled by a number of relatively simple things. The following is a brief discussion on only one type of illusion; the optical illusion. The main upshot is not simply to conclude that we are stupid and easily fooled, but rather to help us understand our own human limitations before attempting to solve the puzzle of existence.

Quick, count the black dots!   These lines are actually straight!

The ball seems to float!

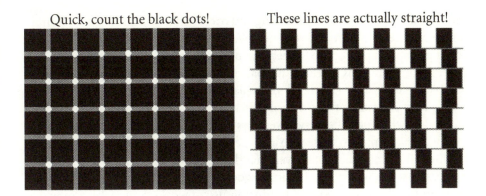

Same size center circles!

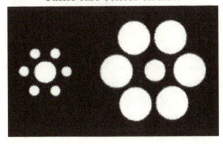

[Images by BWH Ventures, LLC, site designer and maintainer of
http://www.eyetricks.com.]

While we can know intellectually that we are seeing an illusion, something that is not real, we still cannot help but see the illusion. Because of this, we realize that

there is a difference between perceiving and conceiving. Optical illusions illustrate this difference wonderfully. From here we can make a confident generalization about perception being an extremely fast process—a sort of rule of thumb procedure. Optical illusions reveal to us that our perception is not a process that is capable of taking into account all the available sensory data at any given time. If it could, then it wouldn't be so easily tricked by optical illusions. It seems our patched-together perceptual system favors good-enough over exactitude.

Logically, it makes sense that our perception is incapable of taking into account all the possible data, given that doing so would be much too slow of a process. Instead, we find that vision is good-enough at taking images from the surrounding environment and producing useful working models from which the viewer can make decisions.

Optical illusions can be viewed as a way by which we can metaphorically view our imperfect perceptual processes with their pants down. From this perspective, optical illusions can be viewed as system limitations in our perceptual mechanics. For the most part, these limitations do not seem to affect us on a daily basis. In fact, much effort is required to create a top-notch illusion. If anything, that's a testament to the efficiency and effectiveness that is our perceptual norm.

In many ways, what applies to our perceptual system also applies to our broader intellectual apparatus. It's not always reliable. Our sight sometimes deceives us just as our reason might sometimes leave us. Our reason simply can not be trusted when it comes to matters of abstractions that lie beyond our experience. After all, we can't always trust our perceptual experience, so we should be that much more leery when we attempt to abstract away experience altogether.

We have demonstrated that our perceptual system is not infallible. Nevertheless, natural selection did well providing us with the tools it did. We can't expect it to have done more! And perhaps much the same can be said about the reasoning abilities and other tools that natural selection provided us. In other words…OUR REASONING ABILITIES ARE NOT INFALLIBLE! Some examples of our faulty reasoning include…

Faulty Reasoning

Appeal to ignorance   Occurs when a person claims that whatever has not been proved false must be true, and vice versa. For example: UFOs have not been proved False, therefore they must be True.

Special pleading Occurs when a person applies standards, principles, rules, etc. to others while exempting their own interests from those standards, without providing adequate justification for the exemption. For example: That doesn't count against psychic powers. You just don't understand the unique laws of the psychic universe.

Begging the question Occurs when the premises include the claim that the conclusion is true. For example: It's not any Placebo Effect or emotionalism that occurs in Faith Healing. It's the work of God/mystic forces.

Observational selection Occurs when a person counts the hits and forgets the misses. For example: The twenty times that the prophet predicted incorrectly are ignored in favor of the one correct prediction.

Hasty Generalization Occurs when a person draws a conclusion about a population based on a sample that is not large enough. For example: 1 in 5 people can't be Chinese. I see plenty of people in one day, but very rarely do I see a Chinese person. Thus, the 1-in-5 statistic doesn't hold up.

Non sequitur Latin for "it doesn't follow." For example: We will win the war because our leader had a vision/dream of victory.

Post hoc, ergo propter hoc Latin for "it happened after, so it was caused by." For example: Before women got the vote, there were no nuclear weapons. It does not therefore follow that the existence of nuclear weapons are the result of women getting the vote.

Damning the Origin

"Consider the source." This fallacy rejects an argument on account of its undesirable source. However, every statement that Hitler ever made is not false on account of Hitler having said it.

Oversimplification

This fallacy produces a false clarity that misrepresents the actual complexity of the situation or problem. For example: School violence has increased ever since racial segregation was banned. Therefore, segregation should be reintroduced.

Meaningless question

Occurs when a question is rationally meaningless. For example: What happens when an irresistible force meets an immovable object? This question is self-contradictory (an irresistible force precludes an immovable object and vice-versa) and therefore the question is meaningless.

False dichotomy

Occurs when two false extremes are considered in place of a continuum of possibilities. A familiar example: "If you want better public schools, you have to raise taxes. If you don't want to raise taxes, you can't have better schools." A third alternative is that you could spend the existing tax money more efficiently.

Slippery slope

Predicting without justification that one step in a process will lead unavoidably to a second, generally undesirable step. For example: If our First Amendment is compromised in a particular instance, then more and more rights will be taken away from us, until all of our First amendment rights disappear. This is also equivalent to the "Domino Theory" of the Vietnam War era whereby it was argued that if SE Asia was lost to the communists, then eventually the entire world would become communist.

Confusion of Correlation & Causation	The Concise Oxford Dictionary defines correlation as "mutual relation between two or more things" and causation as "causing or producing an effect." For example: More college grads are gay than non-grads, therefore college makes people gay.
Straw man	Occurs when a person simply ignores a person's actual position and substitutes a distorted, exaggerated or misrepresented version of that position to make it easier to attack. For example: Presidential candidate Smith voted against Proposition Spend-on-Military. If candidate Smith had his way, our country would be defenseless.
Suppressed evidence	Occurs when a person intentionally omits relevant data. This is often difficult to detect since we frequently have no way of knowing that we haven't been told the whole truth. For example: Was the "prophecy" made before or after the event?

These examples of faulty reasoning should be kept in mind while reading *The Self-Writing Universe*. After all, criticism can be likened to an environment just as an idea can be likened to an organism. May only the most fit survive!

But for now, we're just falling, falling into a land of…

Puzzles and Contradictions

Let's descend for a moment into what I like to call the Threshold of Nonsense. This is a land of illogic and riddles, contradiction and paradox. This is a strange land we'll be visiting, and I don't blame you if you choose not to follow (but of course you want to). Just remember, clutch firmly upon your sense of humor and hold on to it tightly.

Let's consider the predicament that we are really in, as wonderfully described by Einstein and Leopold Infeld:

> In our endeavor to understand reality we are somewhat like a man trying to understand the mechanism of a closed watch. He sees the

face and the moving hands, even hears its ticking, but he has no way of opening the case. If he is ingenious he may form some picture of a mechanism which could be responsible for all the things he observes, but he may never be quite sure that his picture is the only one which could explain his observations. He will never be able to compare his picture with the real mechanism and he cannot even imagine the possibility of the meaning of such a comparison. (as appearing in Poundstone's *Labyrinths of Reason*)

Part of the problem is that we're trapped in the system that we're trying to describe—so that, if the universe was a watch, then we would be among its gears.

When considering the puzzle that we find ourselves trapped in, we also find that we are limited by the type of logic that we are forced to use and rely on to even describe the puzzle at all. In this regard, consider the distinction between *deductive reasoning* and *inductive reasoning*. Of these two types, it is only deductive reasoning that provides us with any degree of certainty. A famous example of deductive reasoning is:

> All men are mortal
> Socrates is a man
> Therefore, Socrates is mortal.

The logic here is plain. If the premises are true, then so is the conclusion. It's straightforward and definitional. The one catch, of course, is that we cannot escape making assumptions as to what are valid premises. For one thing, are we not assuming that *all men really are mortal*? How do we really know that? Many men are still milling about upon this planet, quite alive and well, thank you very much. How do we know that technology will never advance to such an extent that mortality becomes obsolete (in which case all those men alive today are examples of men who are, in fact, not mortal)? In a similar vein, let's consider a not-so-well-known variation of the Socrates example:

> All fish are smelly
> Socrates is a fish
> Therefore, Socrates is smelly.

While the conclusion here might follow with certainty from the premises, nothing relevant is being demonstrated. In other words, we are free to make the premises as absurd as we might like. And sometimes we simply don't know when a premise is really absurd or not. Consider the axiom "a straight line may be drawn between any two points." While this axiom may seem plainly correct, science now tells us that space-time is actually curved—implying that any line, no matter what, cannot help but be curved also. So then, if we want to insist that "a straight line may be drawn between any two points" is undeniably true, then according to what are we making that claim? We're not making that claim according to this world as it's presently understood.

The deductive argument pays no mind to what is being deduced. It's a mindless algorithm. Accordingly, deductive arguments (whether logical or mathematical) are quite limited as to the kind of knowledge they can provide. If we can be certain of the premises, then we can be certain of the conclusion. However, how often can we really be certain of the premises?

The other type of reasoning is that of *inductive reasoning*. And induction is the type of reasoning that we use to reach the initial premises. It's safe to say every single man that anyone has ever met, in all of history, has been mortal. We therefore induce that ALL MEN ARE MORTAL. Similarly, we might notice that all ravens so far seen in the history of the world have been black. So then, is it not safe to assume that ALL RAVENS ARE BLACK? Since the sun has risen each and every morning ever remembered, are we not safe to assume that THE SUN WILL RISE TOMORROW (assuming for the moment that we're not living on one of the earth's poles)?

We want to say yes. The intuitive pull here is exceptionally strong. That's because all men, so far, have ultimately died, and all ravens, so far, have turned out to be black, and each day, so far, has had a sunrise.

The upshot, however, is that there's no necessity to any of this. Technology might prove capable of making man immortal (an unbearable thought, in my opinion). White ravens might turn out to be exceptionally elusive, although very real nonetheless. And as far as the sun goes, well, one day (hopefully not too soon) our grand flame of a star will flicker for one last time. Once that happens, there will be no such thing as a sunrise tomorrow.

Notice that it isn't proper to actually reject inductive reasoning. Perhaps, sadly, it's all we have to work with. We cannot make deductions (even in a formal system of mathematics) until after we make what amounts to an induction (the axioms used as the starting point). That's a horribly painful, unavoidable paradox, demonstrating yet another obvious limitation in our human reasoning. But still, we only have what we were given by nature to work

with, and all we can really do is make observations regarding our rational shortcomings and manage the best we can.

Consider too the idea of avoiding contradictions. You see, much of logic and reason is contingent upon the demand to avoid contradictions and paradoxes at all cost. Well, is it really that obvious that what we might take to be a contradiction is universally considered contradictory? How do we really know that our logic and way of defining things is the only way of doing such?

The answer to these questions hinges upon whether or not our logic is necessary, and that's precisely what we cannot possibly know. In order to determine that our logic was necessary, we would have to devise some sort of meta-logic to look at logic outside of logic. However, the only way to prove that our new meta-logic was necessary, would be to devise a meta-meta-logic, and so forth and so on, infinitely and forever, world without end. To avoid this infinite regress, a valid form of meta-reasoning must have a demonstrable Buck Stops Here, rendering a meta-meta to be impossible. This, alas, is much easier said than done.

So then, let's agree that our reason is far from perfect, and that if our reason were a diamond, then that diamond would have many a flaw. And some of these flaws, for want of a better analogy, are referred to as contradictions and paradoxes.

The difference between a contradiction and a paradox is quite subtle. A contradiction is something that one tries to avoid, while a paradox is something that one cannot possibly avoid. For example, a conclusion of 1=Ø in a mathematical equation is something that can and should be avoided. That's because it's definitionally meaningless to assert that a 1 can be a Ø when in fact it's not a Ø, it's a 1. This sort of contradiction is very similar to a "married bachelor" or a "squared-circle", things that, by definition, are self-refuting and impossible. However, there are other types of contradictions, typically dealing with self-reference, that don't share this sense of impossibility. A typical example is "this statement is false," whereby if the statement is indeed false, then it's actually making a true statement about itself, and if the statement is true, then it's wickedly making a false statement about itself after all.

A paradox is typically thought of as something that appears contradictory and true at the same time. While "A = not-A" is logically impossible when precise symbols are used, it is a fact of nature that a half-eaten apple is both an apple and not-an-apple. For all intents and purposes, a half-eaten apple represents a paradox—although not a typical one—because two contradictory notions (an "apple" and a "not-an-apple") appear to be true at one and the same time.

Vagueness and Paradox

Vagueness is all over of the place. It's in the world and it's in the words we use to describe the world. Such vagueness, according to typical true-false logic at least, shouldn't exist at all. But, in actuality, such vagueness occurs constantly. When, precisely, does day become night? Or a boy become a man? Or a member of the middle-class become a member of the upper-middle-class? You get the idea.

Famed English mathematician Bertrand Russell correctly identified the problem of vagueness when he stated the following: "the law of the excluded middle [A or not-A] is true when precise symbols are employed but it is not true when symbols are vague, as, in fact, all symbols are." While it is typically believed that something can only be A or not-A, such is not always the case. In fact, it's easy enough to provide a consistent argument "proving" A is not-A. This is known as the Sorites Paradox.

Assumption: A chair contains molecules.

> Throw out 5% of the chair's molecules. Is it still a chair? Yes.
> Throw out 5% more. Is it still a chair? Sort of.
> After enough molecules are thrown out of the chair, the chair turns into a non-chair, or similarly a full head of hair turns bald, or a stack of hay becomes not a stack, or an apple becomes not-an-apple.

The funny thing about Sorites Paradoxes is that they are empirically verifiable. Take enough bites out of an apple and eventually it's no longer an apple. I don't believe our observable reality is at fault in making seamless transitions difficult to describe logically. Rather, I think fault lies with the black-and-white language our logic employs.

Without question, Sorites Paradoxes reveal how our descriptions of things can be vague. Sorites Paradoxes are not particularly good examples, however, of interesting paradoxes. After all, they are mainly descriptive in nature and their implied contradictions can be easily sorted out on a timeline such that at one point there's clearly an apple while at another point there's clearly no longer an apple. It's just the in-between that's truly vague and puzzling, but not necessarily contradictory. For a much more interesting class of paradox, consider the following self-referential paradoxes:

- A Cretan says, "Cretans always lie." If this statement is true, then the Cretan is telling the truth even though Cretans always lie.

- A bumper sticker says trustfully, "DON'T TRUST ME." If we follow the bumper sticker's advice, then we are forced to trust it by *not* trusting it.

- A barber claims to shave all and only those men in town who do not shave themselves. He therefore both shaves and does not shave himself.

- Socrates: "What Plato is about to say is false." Plato: "Socrates has just spoken truly."
  Note that if Socrates had spoken truly, then Plato's statement must be false. But if Plato's statement is false, that means Socrates wasn't telling the truth.

- "This statement is a lie." The Philosopher W.V. Quine has reformulated this simple self-referential statement to the perhaps logically more precise, ""yields falsehood, when appended to its quotation." yields falsehood, when appended to its quotation." Any which way the idea is meta-phrased, however, it seems to follow that: If the statement is true, then it is both a lie and not a lie.

- Hofstadter observes: "Thiss sentence contains threee errors." On reading it, one's first reaction is, "No, no—it contains two errors. Whoever wrote the sentence can't count." At this point, some readers simply walk away scratching their heads and wondering why anyone would write such a pointless, false remark. Other readers make a connection between the sentence's apparent falsity and its message. They think to themselves, "Oh, it made a third error after all—namely, in counting its own errors." A second or two later, these readers do a double-take, when they realize that if you look at it that way, it seems to have correctly counted its errors and is thus not false, hence contains only two errors, and…"But…wait a minute. Hey! Hmm…" (Hofstadter & Dennett, 1982)

This sentence is false. Wait a second, back up and reconsider. Was that sentence really false? Because if it really is false, then doesn't that mean that "this sentence is false" is true? But if "this sentence is false" is really true, then how can it also be false? In a way, the sentence seems both true and false. Oh, what a nasty, nasty tangle. [Note: I understand that "this sentence is false" lacks a reference and is therefore not a valid paradox, but I still have to write words to entertain as well as enlighten, right?—so "this sentence is false" really is false, according to the context I just provided…—hey, wait!]

All the preceding examples are different variations of self-referential paradoxes. A self-referential paradox is basically a contradiction that seems valid in spite of it being a contradiction. In truth, most contradictions are hopelessly uninteresting, e.g., a "squared-circle" and a "married bachelor" are simply meaningless (P.D. Ouspensky's belief in an infinite square-circle not withstanding). Nothing can or will ever follow from such confusion. Yet, not all contradictions are like that. For example, self-referential paradoxes can take the form of A and not-A. They are both true and not-true. Self-referential paradoxes are like a finger that somehow manages to point at itself. And that, to say the least, is quite interesting.

People have long been quick to dismiss paradoxes as simply cute and harmless, as just so much playing with words. The assumption is that paradoxes are intrinsically problems with wording, and that once the wording is better formulated, then the problem will be untangled and resolved. Typically, the assumption that every problem has a unique and reliable solution is a valid assumption to make. Consider the story about the three salespeople at a convention who share a room at the same hotel. In this story, the room costs $30, so each salesperson contributes $10. Later, the desk clerk realizes that the three salespeople should have only been charged $25, not $30, and so sends the bellhop to their room with the $5 change. Now the bellhop, evidently not wishing to split $5 three ways, decides to pocket two of the dollars and return only the remaining $3. So then, at this point each salesperson originally paid $10 for the room, then was returned $1, so that each spent only $9 for the room. Notice that with the three salespeople spending a combined $27 for the room, and with the bellhop pocketing $2, we have $29 accounted for. Hmm…But we originally started out with $30. What happened to that missing dollar?

The solution to this puzzle is not that mathematics is intrinsically paradoxical and unworkable. Rather, the most elegant resolution comes by way of re-assessing the initial financial situation. In the story we are mistakenly led to believe that from the original $30, $27 was spent, and in addition, $2 was pocketed by the bellhop. Instead, the $2 pocketed by the bellhop actually came out of the $27 spent. There really is no "missing" dollar at all: $27 was spent ($25 for the room, and $2 pocketed by the bellhop) and $3 was returned. See how it's just a problem with wording after all (not mathematics)? This is a wonderful example of words being used for purposes of chaos and confusion (ah, my old friends—hey, come to think of it they still owe me $2!), and how disturbingly effective they can be at doing just that. There are many other examples of easily resolvable word-contradictions. The fact that I'm currently caught in a trance-like dilemma whereby I both want and don't want a slice of steak-and-fries gourmet pizza is easily explained by defining "I" as a conglomeration of conflicting desires. The fact that zebras are both white and black at one and the same time is easily sorted out with the concept of stripes. The fact that a photon is a particle and that a photon is also a wave is at least somewhat resolved by explaining how a photon is never actually observed to be both a particle and wave at the same time.

All the same, such neat and tidy solutions to otherwise head-scratching (if not out-and-out butt-scratching) problems are not always available. Indeed, the problem posed by paradoxes has grown surprisingly complex and infuriating over the years. In the early 20th century, Bertrand Russell discovered a paradox involving sets (as in mathematical sets). You see, there are two types of sets. The ordinary type of set, like "the set of all poodles," does not contain itself as a member. That's because "the set of all poodles" is itself not a poodle. The other type of set, however, does contain itself. Consider "the set of all things except poodles." If we were to methodically list all the things contained within this set we would invariably find "the set of all things except poodles." That's because "the set of all things except poodles" is itself not a poodle. In general, the idea of sets runs surprisingly deep, impacting our very experience of the world. Even the concept of "trees" can be thought of as an abstracted set of specific trees, like apple, maple, fir, or elm.

So far, this should all seem intuitive enough. However, we run into problems as soon as we start asking questions about the set of all ordinary sets—e.g., is "the set of all ordinary sets" a member of itself? Well, this is most puzzling. After all, an ordinary set, by definition, cannot be a member of itself. Yet, if all we're doing is grouping all these ordinary sets and saying "alright, these are the sets that we're talking about," well, why should that be prohibited? So let's say that we have a "set of all ordinary sets." Now is it a member of itself? There's no answer to this! That's because if a "set of all ordinary sets" is a member of itself, then it cannot be ordinary, but it has to be ordinary since that's what it's a set of. The 20th century philosopher and computer scientist Douglas Hofstadter calls this sort of thing a "strange loop." It's like a finger trying to point at itself.

Russell didn't care for the idea of formal set theory leading to something as ridiculous as a finger pointing at itself. To circumvent this, he teamed up with mathematician Alfred North Whitehead to create a type of formal mathematics, called the *Principia Mathematica*, with the goal of banishing all traces of self-reference from logic, set theory, and number theory. Now, while it may be easy to spot any and all instances of "this sentence is false" and declare them meaningless, there are other variations of that sentence, such as "the next statement is false" and "the previous statement spoke truly" that appear to create the finger-pointing-at-itself problem, but without either statement being directly self-referential. Well, that's precisely the sort of thing that needed to be banished. So then, to get rid of these incongruities, Russell and Whitehead, in essence, constructed an infinitely tall meta-logic, a sky-scraper really, that positioned "the next statement is false" and "the previous statement spoke truly" on different floors so that they could no longer point to each other (kind of like separating two unruly children by telling one to go upstairs and the other to go downstairs). Well, this attempt proved a failure—and all due to the efforts of just one man.

In 1931, Austrian mathematician and logician Kurt Gödel proved a formalism-destroying theorem that demonstrated that mathematical statements existed for which no systematic procedure could determine whether they were true or false. Russell and Whitehead's *Principia Mathematica* was Gödel's primary target, but the proof actually applied to any and all formal systems. His theorem essentially revealed that the full power of human mathematical reasoning ultimately eludes the capture of formal rigor. The point being that any formal mathematical system, no matter how powerful and brilliant, cannot help but fall victim to an inability at proving its own consistency. Not only was it found that "holes" existed for any formal axiomatic system, but it was also demonstrated that no axiomatic system could produce all number-theoretic truths, that is unless the system was inconsistent.

Gödel showed that a formal system of mathematics cannot prove its own self-consistency without first being inconsistent. In other words, he showed that any formal system attempting to prove its own self-consistency will forever be incomplete—will forever chase after its own tail. He showed that Russell's and Whitehead's *Principia Mathematica*—a formal attempt to rid mathematics of paradox—was itself paradoxical!

How did Gödel do this? Well, he presented a type of mathematical formula that referred back upon itself. If we were to read his mathematical formula in English, it would be something like the following: "this formula is unprovable in Formal System S." It's the self-referential aspect of any formal system attempting to prove its own consistency that turns out to be problematic.

A simple and mostly accurate way of looking at this is with the analogy of a dog chasing after its own tail. In this example, Gödel's formula can be viewed

as a sort of abstract rendition of the very real, spatio-physical problems that a dog encounters when it tries to catch its tail. Now, perhaps this analogy may be confusing to some as, on occasion, some dogs really can "catch" their tail (in which case he'll promptly bite at it for reasons perhaps not even known to dog-spelled-backwards). Instead, then, let's consider the analogy of a finger, once again, attempting to point at itself. For reasons due to both physics and logic, it's quite impossible for that finger to "loop around" in such a way as to point at its own tip. Well, the same sort of thing is going on with Gödel's formula. It's impossible for any formal system to prove its own consistency (or "catch its own tail," or "point at itself"). That's because the formal system is its own self, just like a finger is its own self, and thus cannot escape its own self to either validate itself or point at itself.

Gödel's theorem demonstrates a basic sort of truth—a truth that, although seemingly self-evident (especially when thought of as a finger pointing at itself), still manages to take us by surprise. It demonstrates a natural sort of limitation that is built into any formal system—a limitation arising whenever a formal system attempts to point back upon itself to prove its own consistency. Because Gödel's insight was so deep, it has inspired many a speculative interpretation (even being advocated by some, most notably the famed physicist Roger Penrose, as a sort of metaphysical distinction between awareness and process). While interpretations can be fun, they can also be deceptive. I want the reader to realize that Gödel's theorem is no more or less profound than the image of a finger trying to point back at itself. And by saying this, I don't believe that I'm taking anything away from Gödel's brilliant insight. In my opinion, the most brilliant of thoughts are what scratch at the most basic of truths.

In addition, mathematician Alan Turing demonstrated that if an imaginary list could be devised that includes every conceivable number, then that list could be used to discover the existence of other numbers which could not possibly be present anywhere in the list. As the list theoretically contains all computable numbers, it follows that the new numbers must therefore be uncomputable. By definition, an uncomputable number is a number that cannot be generated by a finitely defined mechanical procedure (i.e., a computation as performed by a computer), even through an infinite number of steps. [According to this definition, the infinitely long *pi* string is considered computable.] Turing showed that uncomputable numbers had to exist which could not be finitely defined by some formal procedure. The upshot is that Turing's proof, like Gödel's, showed that even formal mathematics cannot avoid paradox and inexactitude.

Douglas Hofstadter, cognitive scientist and famed author of *Gödel, Escher, Bach*, summarized the situation as follows: "Undecidable propositions run through mathematics like threads of gristle that criss-cross a steak in such a dense way that they cannot be cut out without the entire steak being destroyed."

Paradoxes, then, are not considered a good thing. They represent the "gristle" of human reason. Paradoxes suggest that the Law of non-Contradiction is not Absolute; sometimes things cannot be neatly divided into either class *A* or class *not-A*. "This statement is a lie," can neither be categorized as true nor false. It is neither true nor false and it is both true and false at one and the same time. Paradoxes virtually shimmer with an inner conflict. Is it true or not-true? A paradox is somehow neither and both at the same time.

Self-referential paradoxes work as a sort of limiting device (i.e., a point of no return) for our knowledge. Gödel showed that any formal system is incapable of validating itself in a complete and non-arbitrary manner. My opinion is that this same limiting device can be used ontologically, meaning that the universe itself (outside of merely our perceptions and knowledge of it) was probably forced into paradox as its beginning point. Note that a paradox is non-regressive, meaning that infinite regresses are rendered impossible. A paradox is its own natural stopping/starting point. In other words, a paradox possesses the exact sort of qualities we would be looking for in a default necessity. The comforting thing about paradoxes is that once we find one, we know that we are at the end of the road of our conceptual understanding. [More on this later...☺]

Quantum Mechanics and Paradox

The concept of paradox takes center stage in any discussion on quantum mechanics. Let's begin this stripped down discussion on quantum mechanics by first considering the "uncertainty principle." This principle states that in any given instant the more precisely a quantum position is determined, the less precisely its momentum is known, and vice versa. For example, if you want to get a measurement of a small thing, e.g. a neutron, it's impossible to get an exact position of that neutron so as to take the measurement without interfering with its position. You can smash it to determine where it's at, but that would destroy its momentum. You can have its picture taken, but then the

photons from the camera's light will clobber the neutron sending it scooting off into an entirely different direction than pictured.

To an extent, this side of quantum mechanics is quite reasonable. Small stuff affects small stuff. However, then there's the "wave-particle duality" and when we're talking about this duality we're no longer talking about anything that's reasonable (at least as typically defined). The wave-particle duality suggests that there may be two mutually incompatible ways to describe certain events. Classically, a beam of light is to be considered as either a wave or as a particle; one way or the other, but not both. Makes sense. Well, turns out that when dealing with an atom it is not at all like a wave. Turns out that the atom is not at all like a solid particle either.

Let's say that we have some sort of a gun that can shoot out one electron at a time. Let's further say that our target is a phosphorescent screen that glows when struck by electrons (e.g., a TV tube). Our goal is to find out whether these electrons are either waves or particles. To that end, we place a removable wall in front of our target—a wall containing two vertical slits parallel to one another. If the electron is a particle, then we should see two vertical stripes on our glowing targets—the two stripes representing billiard ball-type particles passing through the slits. On the other hand, if the electron is a wave, then we should see two new waves radiating from the other side of each slit. And in-between those new waves, we should see an interference pattern, which is the area where the two new waves overlap. The wave pattern is reinforced wherever wave peaks overlap other wave peaks and is canceled out wherever wave peaks meet wave troughs. The difficult thing about this thought experiment is that we already know what happens—and the astonishing results are what quantum mechanics is all about. In a nutshell, when both slits are open, the electron acts like a wave—producing an interference pattern. However, if we decide to close one of those slits, then invariably that same electron will act like a particle—producing a single vertical stripe on the other side. So in some respects, an electron is neither/both like a wave nor/and like a particle. The rhetoric on how best to interpret this scenario is hereby paid homage to in the following extremely condensed manner:

Many Worlds: An electron, when faced with its either/or choice (to behave like a *wave*, or to behave like a *particle*) forces reality to split off into two separate worlds, one world for *either*, and another world for *or*. As you can imagine, this splitting would happen *always* and *infinitely*.

Awareness: Another view, quite heavy on rhetoric and quite popular due to its mystical implications, is that an electron has *no characteristics whatsoever* until viewed.

Positivism: A third view, the standard view, suggests that it's quite senseless to talk about such things (whether an electron is really like *this*, or really like *that*) as, after all, science's job is to perform experiments and not to give interpretations.

"Optical Illusions" and Paradox

We've already seen how optical illusions can be viewed as an analogy to our cognitive limitations. Now, let's take that line of reasoning a step or two further…

Young or old woman?

[Image by BWH Ventures, LLC, site designer and maintainer of http://www.eyetricks.com.]

Quantum mechanics and optical illusions share certain very interesting characteristics. As in the example of the above Young/Old Woman portrait, an optical illusion can be two things at once, either a young woman or an old woman, causing us to flip back and forth between the two interpretations. Giving it a little more thought, we realize that the picture really is both a picture of a young woman and a picture of an old woman, equally, at one and the same time. It's our patched-together perceptual system that can't see the optical illusion for what it is: a picture of a young woman and a picture of an old woman simultaneously. Our patched-together perceptual system corrupts the picture into an either/or, instead of a both.

We can rationally understand that the picture really has two faces at once even though our perceptual abilities limit us to seeing only one face at a time. Despite the fact that evolution did not equip us with a perceptual system capable of seeing both faces at once, we can understand that the picture really shows both faces equally.

The nature of existence might very well have multiple interpretations, like how some people are convinced that the world is strictly material, while others are convinced that the world is strictly mental. My supposition is that those multiple interpretations might still be party to a singular explanation, on a deeper level operating on an entirely separate contextual basis. The problem is that the deeper levels of existence (like the wave/particle duality of quantum mechanics) seem to suggest an *and* while we're stuck interpreting things as an *either/or*. We say that it's either a wave or a particle, but not both. Or we say that quantum mechanics is either observer-dependent, or that it objectively splits off into many unseen worlds.

Well, I think there's a very good chance that we can't comprehend a wave/particle duality in much the same way that we can't see the young and old woman simultaneously in the optical illusion. We have conceptual limits. In the case of the wave/particle duality, we have a word for the situation and it's not "optical illusion." That word is "paradox." And what I intend to drive home to you is that a paradox can represent the limits of our reasoning abilities much like an optical illusion can represent the limits of our perceptual abilities.

Quite frankly, much of the problem is that our interpretations of a deeper level of existence are limited by our evolutionarily patched-together and imperfect reasoning abilities. But, thank goodness, we do have a guide-marker—a light in the darkness. And that light is in fact paradox, such that whenever we meet with a paradox (think Gödel), we can find comfort in the knowledge that we are at the limits of our conceptual understanding and we know that we cannot go further. Seriously, I advise you start thinking this way, because the situation we're stuck in is not going to change anytime soon. You might as well adapt your psychology accordingly. If we think of a paradox as a good thing, as an end of the road, it just makes things easier. In other words—adapt to the world, don't try to make the world adapt to you (it won't work anyway).

I firmly believe that there is a singular explanation for existence, not multiple explanations. I believe that this singular explanation has its own fundamental contextual basis, on a Buck Stops Here level. And I believe that the best way to describe this singular explanation is as a Self-Writing Universe. I also believe that we can somewhat comprehend the reason why the Universe is Self-Writing, although the reason is paradoxical. We therefore know we're at the "end of the road."

That our evolutionarily hard-wired brains are ill-equipped at understanding the foundations of existence is axiomatic. We are a piece of the puzzle we're trying to solve, and it is ourselves who don't quite fit right. When we try to comprehend the picture in its entirety all we see is paradox. That's *our* problem, not the picture's problem! We are the ones who must adapt and make-do.

"Meaning" and Paradox

> "When I use a word," Humpty Dumpty said in rather a scornful tone. "It means just what I choose it to mean—neither more or less."
> "The question is," said Alice, "whether you can make words mean so many different things."
> "The question is," said Humpty Dumpty, "which is to be master—that's all."
>
> **Lewis Carroll (1832—1898)**

The notion of a deep, dark, mysterious meaning of "meaning" lacks meaning. Our meaning is often vague, inexact, and best exemplified by rule-of-thumb methodology. We got a glimpse of this when we discussed the Sorites Paradoxes.

Take the simple word *cup*. That word takes into account a complex range of "thing-identification." A "thing" is identified with the label *cup* when all or some of the following apply: (1) the shape and configuration—e.g., has handle or does not have handle; (2) the material of which it's made; (3) the purpose to which it's used; and (4) where it might be located. When (1) through (4) are matched up in such a way that the label *cup* seems more appropriate than that of *bowl, mug,* or some other label, then that "thing" in question is appropriately identified as a *cup*—or at least, *more a cup than a bowl.* Some "things" are going

to better represent a *cup* than other "things"; and it's possible that some "thing *x*" may well be described as 50% a *cup*, and 50% a *bowl*.

As another example consider the label *vegetable*. This label applies to certain things better than others. I think the best way to describe this state of affairs might be by way of Lotfi Zadeh's "fuzzy sets." If we treat *vegetable* as a member of a fuzzy set, we assign grades of membership to this set by means of quotients between zero and one. Since a *sparrow* absolutely does not belong under the category of *vegetable* we therefore assign it a value of ∅. A *carrot*, on the other hand, is assigned a value of 1. All the same, there are occasions when our meaning is fundamentally unclear. A study in 1969 by Battig & William Montague reported the following results when 270 students from the University of Maryland and 172 students from the University of Illinois were given 56 different category headings—including that of *vegetable*—and asked to list as many examples as they could think of for each category.

The ten most frequently mentioned examples of *vegetables* were:

(1) carrot, (2) pea, (3) corn, (4) bean, (5) potato, (6) tomato—also ranked #15 under fruit, (7) lettuce, (8) spinach, (9) asparagus, (10) broccoli.

This study demonstrates the transient nature of our meaning. You see, a tomato is technically a fruit because it has seeds, yet a tomato is more often than not used as a vegetable (e.g., in a salad), and not as a fruit (e.g., as a dessert). Therefore, our meaning is often-times imprecise, and on these occasions it is appropriate to say, "such and such is more *x* than *not-x*."

Accordingly, a meaningful statement must be *more accurate than inaccurate*, and that is at times the best we can do. A tomato should not necessarily be thought of as a fruit—even though it has seeds—because it is actually used as a vegetable. It may be defined as a fruit, but this definition has little to do with the necessary meaning of the word *fruit*, which includes both "has seeds" and "how used." Similarly, a sea-horse's gender is defined by who carries the eggs and who carries the sperm, yet functionally it is the sperm-carrier that becomes pregnant and gives birth. Wacky?

Not really. Our interpretations and meanings simply have a way of becoming hardened and codified. We compress reality into the rule that only females give birth, and that's just not true. Reality has a slippery way of squirming away from most hard and fast classifications. One of the great rules is that there is always exceptions to the rule. Not all values need be ascribed as either 1 or ∅;

sometimes, like with a tomato or a sea-horse, our meaning is such that neither 1 nor ∅ should properly be ascribed.

The statement "A = not-A" might be logically impossible when precise symbols are used, but a half-eaten apple sure seems to be both an apple and not-an-apple. And a tomato sure seems to be both a vegetable and a fruit. And a male sea-horse sure seems to be as much female as male. For all intents and purposes, a half-eaten apple, a tomato, and a sea-horse represent types of paradoxes because two contrarian notions (an "apple" and a "not-an-apple," "a vegetable" and "a fruit" and "a male" and "a female") appear to be true at one and the same time.

Fuzziness is a way to offer descriptive accounts to the following questions: Where is the line that divides day from night? When is a glass "full"? When is a banana "ripe"? When is a person "rich"? If you hack off one of its legs, is the object still a "chair"? How about if you hack off two legs? When is something "obscene"? You get the drift.

"Fuzziness" is first and foremost a useful way of talking about things, and is probably best viewed as an interpretive addition to probability theory—much like *punctuated equilibrium* can be viewed as an interpretive addition to natural selection theory. It's important to note that fuzziness' usefulness stems from its apparent ability to "match up" with the way the world works.

I think the assumption that all values *can be* or *should be* ascribed as either 1 or ∅ is simply not experientially demonstrable. That assumption represents an "ought" from an "is" and does not appropriately reflect the messiness of the world we live in. It reflects a made-up world, a false world, a lollipop world that doesn't admit of paradox. No thanks! I'd rather take reality as it is, thank you very much, rather than as others might wish it to be.

Memes and WorldViews

The fuzzy meanings we occasionally use to categorize and understand our messy world leads me to the subject of *memes*. The concept of "memes" has been used and abused in recent years, becoming a sort of intellectualist cliché. Originally intended as an interesting analogy linking the stuff of the mind with the stuff of biology, the concept of memes has mutated its way into becoming something much more. When viewed strictly as an analogy, the concept of memes suggests that a mind is to a brain as a meme is to a gene so that mental stuff (like ideas, scientific theories, popular songs, jokes, mathematical formulas,

etc.) is in fact a "meme." The analogy further suggests that a meme can "survive" and even "flourish" by replicating itself from mind to mind like a virus. Trouble ensues when the analogy is hardened into a literal truism—the primary difficulty being that there's no such thing as an objective, scientifically observable "meme" to study. However this may be, a "meme," if used with its originally intended analogical spin, remains a useful shorthand way of discussing an idea's viability and its probability for success among competing ideas.

So memes are basically ideas, and they compete in a market-place of ideas. Those ideas that survive and prosper become popular while those that fail simply whither away. As a self-referential example, a major impediment for the acceptance of this book's meme is that it does not come from a famous or influential person. The all-too-human factor here concerns the very fabric of the type of civilization we live in and how one communicates inside of it, and how others filter out the flood of incoming information to make sense of it.

Any given community has, by the nature of how things work, its share of the elite, the mediocre, and the nondescript. Society's filtering system, influenced and enhanced by the modern mass media, weeds out the perceived mediocre and nondescript presenting only the elite to the outside world (leaving an at-best community-wide recognition for the rest). [Notice, however, that this system is far from perfect as there are many examples of an obscure member of "the rest" being identified by later generations as "genius."]

So, the odds against this book's meme surviving, let alone thriving are assumed to be staggering. However, this book's meme is yet interesting enough (so it is claimed) to warrant a studied exposition, even if coming from a complete unknown. Quite frankly, the fact that this book's meme is originating from a complete unknown, an absolute outsider to both the scientific and philosophic communities (not to mention the cosmos at large), can be looked upon as a dramatic element to this entire project. It's so easy to read through this book only to reject the project outright—on account of an unknown author. It's so easy to ask "who is this guy? I've never heard of him, he must not know what he's talking about!" But the conflict is that IT'S A VERY FINE MEME.

There are many deep, underlying issues of the world that I would like explained. The resulting explanation, the "Script" meme presented in this book, is basically my own idiosyncratic worldview. Alas, so that you be aware, my worldview is rather *un*original (although there are parts of it that I believe are *quite* original), most of it being little more than warmed-over computationalism and natural selectionism in origin, and decidedly interpretational in scope. The world is not "really" a computer. It's not really even a very "messy" super-computer of networked computers working with smoking parallel processors and tons of RAM. But it can still be thought of as being like a computer, at least in so far as it can be considered an ongoing computational process. And I think the analogy of the world as a computer is the best one we currently have to go by. There's an arbitrariness about this since the "world as a watch" was once a popular analogy in time's past, but now seems passé. And soon enough, I hope, an analogy will come along that's superior to "computer"—but we have to use what we've got. And my feeling is that whatever ultimately replaces "computer" will turn out to be a better, more sophisticated, way of conveying the same underlying idea—much like "computer" trumps "watch."

I understand that our world is probably not really understandable in such a way that our conceptualizations actually "map up" in a linearly perfect way to the external world—at least I don't believe things to be that simple. Instead, I've resigned myself to play a game of paradox-finding and gross approximations.

As mentioned before, when we find a true paradox, we can then comfort ourselves in knowing that we're at the end of our conceptual road. And the only reason I believe that gross approximations are at all reliable and worthy of our attention is because I trust natural selection. We can be reasonably certain that the things we see, hear, smell, taste, and feel are at least grossly approximate to what's actually out there because otherwise how could we as a species have ever survived? If our ancestors' approximations of reality were terribly inaccurate, they would have died out. So we have reason to believe in gross approximations, while at the same time being leery of them, with the understanding that our gross approximations might be grossly inaccurate.

The Script meme, my worldview, interprets the universe to be computational in nature; a sort of giant algorithm deriving much complexity from truly simple beginnings. The idea of complexity arising from out of simplicity is quite secure. One need only look at The Game of Life to understand the general principle. The Game of Life has one rule (visit the website http://abc.net.au/science/holo/lablife.htm, among others, to get a real-time demonstration, or better yet just go to Google or some other search engine and type in "Game of Life": Remember, websites may come and go, but there will always be a search engine!):

> For each cell in the grid, count how many of its eight neighbors are ON. If the answer is two, the cell remains the same (ON or OFF). If the answer is three, the cell is ON regardless of what it was previously. In all other conditions, the cell is OFF.

The Game of Life metaphorically demonstrates the viability of complexity being derivable from a simple rule, specifically a simple computational rule. This rule, this theme, is recursively manipulated leading to complex and unpredictable results. The Mandelbrot set can be viewed as showing much the same thing. (To attain your own supply of Mandelbrot images please visit your nearest search engine).

Both the Game of Life and the Mandelbrot set can be described as arguments by analogy, in essence amounting to little more than a series of interesting pictures on a computer screen that can be interpreted as demonstrating something deep and profound about the nature of reality and how it operates. They metaphorically suggest that a simple recursive algorithm can lead to very complex and unexpected results.

Needless to say, much can be said about the difficulties involved in using arguments by analogy. Nevertheless, if analogies are kept in check, I believe they can be not only powerful rhetorical devices, but also decidedly useful as thought-tools.

As an example of a useful analogy, Plato's shadow-cave conveys his philosophy of Forms as it contrasts with the sensible world's reality by depicting humans looking at shadows on a wall with their backs facing the opening of the cave. So too, Darwin's original argument for natural selection was an extended argument by analogy: the implication running heavy that if selective variation can apply to breeding, then surely something like it must apply to speciation as well. For instance, dogs are a single species, with many variants. In only a few thousand years, both the Chihuahua and the Saint Bernard have been intentionally evolved from the wolf by humans through the manipulation of processes existing in nature. While Darwin's analogy did not rely on a picture-image as did Plato's, it was still highly effective at getting across a very deep, abstract idea.

Obviously, an analogy is not identical to the real thing—it's just a model, a compression, of what we're really interested in knowing about. Analogies help us understand something that is far more abstract and difficult to understand than the analogy itself. Mathematical models of the solar system, of atoms, and of black holes are useful for much the same reason.

While mathematics still dominates the scientific world (due in large part to its powerful model-making abilities), computationalism in recent years has become a close second. Occasionally it's suggested that mathematics is incapable of solving anything but the simplest of physical problems. As an example, it might be noted that Isaac Newton was able to calculate the orbit of a planet around a star but neither he nor any of his successors have been able to come up with a reasonable mathematical model for more complicated phenomena like turbulence or evolution. Some have suggested that the limitations of mathematics can be corrected by the program-building of computationalism. Taken to its extremes, as *Mathematica* creator Stephen Wolfran shows, computationalism can be said to obey "the Principle of Computational Equivalency," implying that all processes in the universe are capable of being computed by a Turing machine (or any universal computational device). Of course, such an hypothesis can neither be proven, nor disproven. It's interpretational. I personally believe, however, that we live in a messy universe and the suggestion that it might be computationally clean simply defies my expectations.

Regardless of the extent that one wishes to take the worldview of computationalism, there does seem to be something to it. Examples in nature of computational programs are manifold. For example, the arrangement of seeds in a sunflower can be understood by using Fibonacci numbers (1, 1, 2, 3, 5, 8, 13…), named after the Italian merchant Leonardo Fibonacci of Pisa. Except for the first two numbers, every number in the sequence equals the sum of the previous two. Sunflower heads, like other flowers, contain two families of interlaced spirals—one winding clockwise, the other counterclockwise. The number of seeds and petals are almost always Fibonacci numbers. If viewed as a program that the sunflower is somehow reading, the recurring Fibonacci numbers seemingly make sense.

Other computational examples: Seashells, animal's horns, and the cochlea of the ear are all logarithmic spirals that can be generated using a mathematical constant known as the golden ratio. Mountains and the branching patterns of blood vessels and plants are *fractals*, a class of shapes that exhibit similar structures at different magnifications.

Basically, computationalism compresses two very intuitive ideas: that the universe is mathematical in nature and that the universe is a process. For both of those qualities to be true, for the universe to be both mathematical and procedural, then the universe must operate like a computation, a program. Again, none of what I'm saying is the least bit original. Just planting seeds of thought…

Whether we interpret the universe as "mathematical" or "programmatical," it is still merely a descriptive interpretation. Real-world phenomena are being described in a certain way, but nothing more really follows. Whether the universe is interpreted as either a giant equation or a giant algorithm (and, of course, it might actually be a VERY VERY SMALL equation/algorithm in a yet bigger…), it stands to reason that the universe may very well represent its own

best, most compressed example of itself. It cannot be further "zipped" up and compressed (to save space on the old hard-drive!).

Well, if it's true that our universe cannot be compressed further, it follows that no future complex structures (like "weather," or the "history" that Marx attempted to divine) can be predicted by science even if science fully adopts the computationalist interpretation; in fact there would be no science to speak of when it comes to predicting future states of complex structures. Billions upon billions of iterations can be observed each step of the way as our universe undergoes its algorithmic process, but since our universal system is complex enough to approach true randomness, even knowing exactly where you are at any given step wouldn't help you predict where you will be at in a future step.

So too, it is practically impossible to determine the underlying rules and initial conditions of a cellular automaton (as in The Game of Life) by looking at the deterministic pattern that it generates—especially if the pattern is complex and random. Even if we knew with certainty that some complex process was generated by a cellular automaton with simple rules, that alone would not help us understand what that underlying rule or program might be. Makes you wonder whether we're really any better off now than before you ever heard of computationalism.

And, very pointedly, we will never ever know with certainty that the worldview of computationalism (or any other worldview for that matter) is the real and best interpretation. After all, the universe has long been viewed as a conundrum to be solved by one simple explanation, whether that explanation be matter, mass, energy, time, space, mathematics, points, lines, strings, spirit, mind, ideas, God, machines, motion, vortices, nothing, life, water, earth, or a myriad of other possible interpretations that have all been advocated as the real and best interpretation of the universe at one time or another. It's important to stay humble in these matters and be ever aware that such worldviews are not written in stone, but rather to a large degree are poetry, story-telling, and analogizing.

Well, my overall perspective will not add anything new to the table regarding its inability to predict future behavior. And as already mentioned, my worldview does not even introduce a unique or novel interpretation of the universe. However, I believe that my overall perspective is original when it comes to describing the universe's initial conditions. And this is the main difference distinguishing *The Self-Writing Universe*'s meme from all the others.

Are We *Too* Limited?

Well, with all this talk about our human gullibility and limitations, we reach an obvious and inevitable crisis point. Is it possible in principle for us to ever understand how existence came to be?

It's difficult to fathom why our evolutionary survival should have led to our possessing esoteric reasoning abilities capable of answering such an abstract, otherworldly question as how and why is there existence, instead of nonexistence? Why should we trust anything that our limited minds might offer?

Well, consider that the collective works of Lewis Carroll is nowhere to be found in our evolutionary survival program. In fact, there are a lot of things that seem to have only an indirect relation to our survival program. For instance, our verbal communication and symbol-manipulation abilities provide, in primitive form, an advantage for us over the organisms lacking these skills. However, to suggest that *Alice in Wonderland* therefore follows is an absurdity.

Perhaps the best, if not only, way to resolve this dilemma is to flat-out assume that we live in a world where rich complexity can spring from simple mechanisms. In this regard, natural selection can be viewed as basically a big, dumb mechanism. It churns away, deleting the organisms that can't survive, and saving the organisms that can survive. It's a very simple process, as it must be since there's no one behind the scenes pulling the strings.

Zooming in closer to look at our prehistoric selves, consider how at some point in our evolutionary history our grunts and etchings started to have greater meaning for us. When that happened, it provided us with a distinct advantage—both for us *in general* compared to other species, and for us *in particular* helping those better versed in the art of communication to more effectively woo mates and procreate (your DNA program can't get "saved" unless you pass on your seed!).

The selective mechanism that first allowed for communication and symbol-manipulation in humans was probably a very simple one, predominantly concerned with getting saved in the program of life. This simple saving mechanism, at some point gave us a basic form of verbal communication and symbol-manipulation.

The program of life ran, through us—providing great complexity and sophistication to something that ultimately derived from a very simple rule. And so the end result is that we possess reasoning abilities way beyond the level of what was originally selected. We have already seen how great complexity and sophistication can explode from simple rules, and there's no way of knowing

ahead of time just how much of an explosion has occurred. So, we can only hope for the best and prepare for the worst. But having said that, I am still convinced that the originations of existence is yet possible for us to understand. Natural selection bestowed on us a complex brain. While our brains are prone to gullibility and limitations, they also exemplify the best that the universe has to offer (at least in so far as we know!). It's our duty to simply GO! In spite of it all, in the face of overwhelming odds, we must simply put one step in front of the other and keep going: like the little stream of water that ended up forming the Grand Canyon. The critics and killjoys be damned: let history be our judge. Upshot? We don't know for a fact that we are incapable of solving the puzzle of existence, therefore we must act as though we can solve it and sort out why it turned out to be possible/impossible later!

BYTE TWO:

GOD VS. CHANCE

http://www.philscanlan.net/

The Master had quoted Aristotle: "In the quest for truth, it would seem better and indeed necessary to give up what is dearest to us." And he substituted the word "God" for "truth."

Later a disciple said to him, "I am ready, in the quest for God, to give up anything: wealth, friends, family, country, life itself. What else can a person give up?"

The Master calmly replied, "One's beliefs about God."

The disciple went away sad, for he clung to his convictions. He feared "ignorance" more than death.

Anthony de Mello—*One Minute Wisdom*

The Mystery of Existence

Below are two wonderful excerpts from one of our great thinkers, the American philosopher William James. I simply wish here to get across some of the mystery surrounding the puzzle of existence: and how better to do that than by considering some choice ruminations from a renowned thinker?

How comes the world to be here at all instead of nonentity which might be imagined in its place? Schopenhauer's remarks on this question may be considered classical. "Apart from man," he says, "no being wonders at its own existence. When man first becomes conscious, he takes himself for granted, as something needing no explanation. But not for long; for, with the rise of the first reflection, that wonder begins which is the mother of metaphysics, and which made Aristotle say that men now and always seek to philosophize because of wonder—The lower a man stands in intellectual respects the less of a riddle does existence seem to him...but, the clearer his consciousness becomes the more the problem grasps him in its greatness. In fact the unrest which keeps the never stopping clock of metaphysics going is the thought that the non-existence of this

world is just as possible as its existence. Nay more, we soon conceive the world as something the non-existence of which not only is conceivable but would indeed be preferable to its existence; so that our wonder passes easily into a brooding over that fatality which nevertheless could call such a world into being, and mislead the immense force that could produce and preserve it into an activity so hostile to its own interests. The philosophic wonder thus becomes a sad astonishment, and like the overture to Don Giovanni, philosophy begins with a minor chord."

One need only shut oneself in a closet and begin to think of the fact of one's being there, of one's queer bodily shape in the darkness (a thing to make children scream at, as Stevenson says), of one's fantastic character and all, to have the wonder steal over the detail as much as over the general fact of being, and to see that it is only familiarity that blunts it. Not only that *anything* should be, but that *this* very thing should be, is mysterious! Philosophy stares, but brings no reasoned solution, for from nothing to being there is no logical bridge.

Attempts are sometimes made to banish the question rather than to give it an answer. Those who ask it, we are told, extend illegitimately to the whole of being the contrast to a supposed alternative non-being which only particular beings possess. These, indeed, were not, and now are. But being in general, or in some shape, always was, and you cannot rightly bring the whole it into relation with a primordial nonentity. Whether as God or as material atoms, it is itself primal and eternal. But if you call any being whatever eternal, some philosophers have always been ready to taunt you with the paradox inherent in the assumption. Is past eternity completed? they ask: If so, they go on, it must have had a beginning; for whether your imagination traverses it forwards or backwards, it offers an identical content or stuff to be measured; and if the amount comes to an end in one way, it ought to come to an end in the other. In other words, since we now witness its end, some past moment must have witnessed its beginning. If, however, it had a beginning, when was that, and why?

You are up against previous nothing, and do not see it ever passed into being. This dilemma, of having to choose between a regress which, although called infinite, has nevertheless come to a termination, and an absolute first, has played a great part in philosophy's history…. (William James, 1911)

Ah, James here provides us with a poignant reminder of the dichotomy between non-entity and entity and whether or not there was a "Beginning Point" when entity was somehow favored over its opposite. Below, James describes how it's the stuff out there, of which we are so intricately a part, that makes the recipe behind existence so delicate, so special, so ungraspingly real:

Sight of elephants and tigers at Barnum's menagerie whose existence, so individual and peculiar, yet stands there so intensely and vividly real, as much so as one's own, so that one feels again poignantly the unfathomableness of ontology, supposing ontology to be at all. They *are*, *eodem jure* with myself, and yet I, with my pretensions or at least aspirations to adequately represent the world, can never hope to *sympathize* in a genuine sense of the word with their being. And the want of sympathy is not as in the case of some deformed or loathsome human life, for their being is admirable; so admirable that one yearns to be in some way its sharer, partner or accomplice. Thus their foreignness confounds one's pretension to comprehend the world—while their admirableness undermines the stoic or moral frame of mind in which one says the real meaning of life is *my* action. The great world of life, in no relation with my action, is so real! (William James, 1873)

I hope with these two excerpts from William James that the reader gets a taste of the deep sense of mystery that is the puzzle of existence.

The Master gave his teaching in parables and stories, which his disciples listened to with pleasure—and occasional frustration, for they longed for something deeper.

The Master was unmoved. To all their objections he would say, "You have yet to understand, my dears, that the shortest distance between a human being and Truth is a story."

Another time he said, "Do not despise the story. A lost gold coin is found by means of a penny candle; the deepest truth is found by means of a simple story."

Anthony de Mello, *One Minute Wisdom*

"In the beginning..."

"In the beginning,…." Yeah, we've all heard it before. Now, in this cynical time of post-ironicism (where even irony is often approached with irony), what, really, should we make of the ancient scripts of the universe? Well, before judging these scripts too hastily, let's take a quick look at some of them.

Origin Myths

Perhaps not surprisingly (given the near-infinite range of opinion that people have), there are various *types* of recipes for the universe. These are typically called "Origin Myths." The most fundamental difference between the various Origin Myths is whether or not a "beginning" is assumed. For instance, while some Origin Myths assume a *beginning* to things, other Origin Myths assume *no beginning* at all. [The following is owed in large part to the physicist Marcelo Gleiser's book *The Dancing Universe*.]

1. Creation Myths

Genesis (c. 400 B.C.):

In the Beginning God created the heavens and the earth. The earth was without form and void, and darkness was upon the face of the deep; and the Spirit of God was moving over the face of the waters.

And God said, "Let there be light"; and there was light.

And God saw that light was good; and God separated the light from the darkness.

God called the light Day, and the darkness He called Night. And there was evening and there was morning, one day.

Taoist Myth (*c.* 200 B.C.):

In the beginning there was chaos. Out of it came pure light and built the sky. The heavy dimness, however, moved and formed the earth from itself. Sky and earth brought forth the ten thousand creations, the beginning, having growth and increase, and all of them take the sky and earth as their mode. The roots of Yang and Yin—the male and female principle—also began in sky and earth. Yang and Yin became mixed, the five elements separated themselves from it and a man was formed.

2. "No-Creation" Myths

Hindu *Veda* (*c.* 1200 B.C.):

When neither Being nor Non-Being was
Nor atmosphere, nor firmament, nor what is beyond.
What did it encompass? Where? In whose protection?
What was water, the deep, the unfathomable?
Neither death nor immortality was there then,
No sign of night or day.
That One breathed, windless, by its own energy:
Nought else existed then.
In the beginning was darkness swathed in darkness;
All this was but unmanifested water.
Whatever was, the One, coming into being,
Hidden by the Void,
Was generated by the power of heat.
In the beginning this One evolved,
Became desire, the first seed of mind.

Wise seers, searching writhing their hearts
Found the bond of Being in Non-Being.
Was there a below? Was there an above?…

Who knows truly? Who can declare it?
Whence it was born, whence is this emanation.
By the emanation of this the gods only later came to be.
Who knows whence it has arisen?…

Only He who is its overseer in heights heaven knows.
He only knows, or perhaps He does not know!

3. Modern Variations

Alan Guth and Paul Steinhardt, 1984

> The inflationary model of the universe provides a possible mechanism by which the observed universe could have evolved from an infinitesimal region. It is then tempting to go one step further and speculate that the entire universe evolved from literally nothing.

Heinz Pagels, *Perfect Symmetry*, 1985

> The nothingness "before" the creation of the universe is the most complete void that we can imagine—no space, time, or matter existed. It is a world without place, without duration or eternity, without number—it is what mathematicians call "the empty set." Yet this unthinkable void converts itself into the plenum of existence—a necessary consequence of physical laws. Where are these laws written into the void? What "tells" the void that it is pregnant with a possible universe? It would seem that even the void is subject to law, a logic that exists prior to space and time.

John Archibald Wheeler, 1986

> Existence, the preposterous miracle of existence! To whom has the world of opening day never come as an unbelievable sight? And to whom have the stars overhead and the hand and voice nearby never

appeared as unutterably wonderful, totally beyond understanding? I know of no great thinker of any land or era who does not regard existence as the mystery of all mysteries.

But is the quantum a mystery, too? We know that the way the quantum theory works is no mystery. It is expounded in a hundred texts. But from what deeper principle does its authority and its way of action derive? What central concept undergirds it all? Surely the magic central idea is so compelling that when we see it, we will all say to each other, "Oh how simple, how beautiful! How could it have been otherwise? How could we have been so stupid for so long?"

Upshot

For the sake of argument, let's say that the above Origin Myths are best read as poetry and that as absolutes none of them will do. When we abstract away the unessential from the ancient Origin Myths, we are left with the same conceptual false dichotomy presented by the modern scientific origin theories (myths?): **Either** there was a *beginning* and it all started from some freak quantum disturbance or else God created it, **or** there was *no beginning* and the Universe simply always existed, perhaps in a cyclical series of crunches and bangs. I require a process that actually describes *how* and *why* the existence of the universe (or *anything*, for that matter) unfolded in the first place. I don't think "quantum disturbance" does the Trick. I don't think "always existed" does the Trick. And I don't think "it was God" does the Trick either. So then, what *does* do the Trick? In fact, what even *is* the Trick?

Well, before attempting to answer that question we'll first need to cover some preliminary groundwork. And where better to begin than with the important notion of **assumptions**, as in *first assumptions*. 19th century philosopher Arthur Schopenhauer, in a discussion on the Principle of Sufficient Reason, argued that certain fundamental assumptions will inevitably be *inexplicable*, forever beyond human knowledge:

> Up to a point, explanation "explains things in reference to one another, but it always leaves unexplained something that it presupposes. In mathematics, for example, this is space and time; in mechanics, physics, and chemistry, it is matter, qualities, original forces, laws of nature; in botany and zoology it is the difference of species, and life itself; in history, it is the human race with all its characteristics of thought and will." That which is presupposed is inexplicable. (Schopenhauer)

A sublime example of this sort of inexplicability might turn out to be the notion of existence. As 18th century German philosopher Immanuel Kant put it, "the real contains no more than the possible. A hundred real dollars do not contain a penny more than a hundred possible dollars.… By whatever, and by however many, predicates I may think a thing, nothing is added to it if I add that the thing exists.… Whatever, therefore, our concept of an object may contain, we must always step outside of it in order to attribute to it existence."

What Schopenhauer and Kant are talking about here unveils a very deep and disturbing puzzle. They are suggesting that no matter where you begin, there will always be an inexplicable remainder, a First Assumption that will forever be outside of our intellectual understanding. The question becomes whether it's even possible to have a viable theory of originations that leaves no remainder, no inexplicability. While I think this is possible, we're still in need of some explanation as to *how* it can be possible. To that end, let's consider the following exchange of ideas.

Let's say that you and I are in a debate, and that *your* position in the debate is "Existence must have some sort of script" while *my* position is "Existence Exists and nothing more can be said." Now, it certainly *seems* as though I have defined "existence" to mean "necessary." Furthermore, it certainly *seems* as though I have also defined "necessary" to mean "inexplicable." *My* argument certainly *seems to be* that "If A is necessary, then it is inexplicable and cannot be explained further." Now "A" here can be God, the Universe, Existence, An Accident, or even a Ham Sandwich—it doesn't really matter. The point is that whatever is thought of as necessary must also therefore be thought of as inexplicable. *Your* argument, on the other hand, seems to demand that even if we choose to call "A" necessary, there still must be some way by which "A" came to be necessary (i.e., its *script*).

I could say "how would you even know what a correct Script would be like?" whereupon you could reply "all I'd be looking for is a *reasonable approximation* of the original Script." Well, if this were to be our debate, we would be none too original. For instance, consider the interplay between philosophers Bryan Magee and W.V. Quine in *Men of Ideas* concerning the subject-matter of philosophy:

Magee   Do you include in its field of concern, or do you exclude from it, the age-old questions about how the world got here in the first place, and how life began?

Quine   I exclude these from philosophy. How the world began is a problem for the physicist and astronomer, and of course there have been conjectures from that quarter. How life began is a problem for the biologist, on which he's made notable progress in recent years. Why the world began, or why life began—on the other hand—I think are pseudo questions, because I can't imagine what an answer would look like.

Magee   You think that, because there is no conceivable answer to these questions, they are meaningless questions?

Quine   Yes.

Clearly, Quine is in agreement with defining existence as meaning "necessary" which, in turn, would be the same as meaning "inexplicable" in a philosophical context. Furthermore, he seems to believe that this way of defining things is entirely dependent upon *his* powers of imagination. Hmm. Well, that's a rather ingenious way of avoiding the problem—we can at least grant him that! Nevertheless, *you* can counter Quine with another quote, this from Magee's *The Philosophy of Schopenhauer*:

> Why is there something rather than nothing? That there is anything is not…what one would have expected…"In fact, the balance wheel which maintains in motion the watch of a metaphysic that never runs down is the clear knowledge that the world's non-existence is just as possible as is its existence"—a recognition, as Schopenhauer is quick to point out, which is implicit in any belief in a God as creator of the world; "it infers the world's previous non-existence from its existence; thus, it assumes in advance that the world is something contingent."

> Existence, then, precisely because it is contingent, presents philosophizing man with a problem which is fundamental in a literal sense: it could not have been taken for granted a priori, yet it is prior to all other issues. Indeed, even given the fact of existence, everything else could have been quite other than it is.

With this quote you seem to be suggesting that "existence" is equivalent to "a bunch of stuff" and that instead of "a bunch of stuff," there could have just as easily been "nonexistence" or "not any stuff at all." All the same, I take it that our respective positions at this point are quite clear. Namely, *I'm* stating categorically that the best way to define existence is as "necessarily inexplicable." On the other hand, *you're* saying, "I don't care how you *define* it, just show me how it got to be like that (*possibly*) in the first place." Notice how similar your attitude is to that of Einstein's (in this respect, I'd say you're in quite good company):

I want to know how God created this world. I am not interested in this or that phenomenon. I want to know His thoughts, the rest are details. (Albert Einstein, 1955)

There does seem to be an important difference between your view and Einstein's however. Instead of wanting to know (metaphorically) how "God created this world" you want to know the Script for how "Existence came to exist." My only response to you at this point is the following:

The mind whirls in attempting to imagine how everything could have sprung forth from literally nothing—nothing but a pre-existing fluctuating "false vacuum" governed by nature's ultimately unified force law. If recent theory is on the right course, it seems that the universe is nothing but a nothingness that has elaborated itself. A formless void incubated all being. Can we conceive of this nothingness in any way? Probably not. The mind simply refuses to transcend space-time to reach perfect nonexistence. (Eugene Mallove, *The Quickening Universe*, p.30)

Of course, you might counter that such a view is quite irrelevant. After all, who ever said that we *should* be able to conceive of nonexistence? What does such a thing even mean? Can we even conceive of *existence*? If so, then what does *that* really mean?

I now ask: how can a Script be developed that somehow avoids a First Assumption, an inexplicable remainder? (And I ask this not a moment too soon, by the way. As you'll recall, this question was the sole purpose of what has been, so far at least, our astonishingly friendly exchange of ideas.) With this question, I'm suggesting, strongly, that no matter the basis of the argument (e.g., God, Chance, Universe is Eternal, etc.) there will always be an inexplicable remainder and we'll be no better off than when we started. You counter that the puzzle can indeed be solved, but that it just needs to be looked at correctly (as with any good puzzle). And that, once this puzzle is looked at correctly it will be found that contained within the puzzle is a default necessity—a necessity that writes itself. You suggest that if a thing can be shown to be necessary, and to write itself, well, then that thing would be the very antithesis of an inexplicability. Relative to human conceptual thought, there will be nothing left to explain.
End of debate.

[H]ow can the machinery of the universe ever be imagined to get set up at the very beginning so as to produce man now?

John Archibald Wheeler

If not G, then C?

There's little money to be made in the pursuit of philosophical conundrums. Little hope for material reward, let alone personal edification. Most people, perhaps wisely, follow a life's pathway that produces quantifiable results, not to mention a supportable income. The deepest of philosophical considerations, those questions that were first asked and left unanswered in childhood, get pushed to one side, never resolved, safely ignored and forgotten. Yet, there really are interesting mysteries in this world that can only be explored through what has been traditionally classified as philosophy (not to be confused with modern-day, professional philosophy which happens to be in the midst of an identity crisis). It is my contention that these explorations can be intellectually refreshing and occasionally entertaining; especially when the exploration digs deep into the greatest of all mysteries.

Wheeler's question at the top of this page can be found peering out of every nook and cranny of this book. I like how Wheeler specifically uses the word "machinery." I think it represents the appropriate way of viewing the subject of originations. Not because the universe should be necessarily thought of as a machine, but because it assumes that the universe can be understood. And why should we assume otherwise?

So then, allow me to ask a few basic questions. Where did the universe come from? How did it get here? What are its ingredients and how did those ingredients get put together? In other words, what is the universe's Script and how did the set of instructions for that Script initially come to be?

Okay, so those are the questions. Now what? Is it time to shrug our collective shoulders and safely forget about the whole deal once again? Are we to assume that such questions are only so much metaphysical nonsense? Are they to be regarded as unanswerable *a priori*? After all, how could we ever even know that we had a correct answer even if we were staring at it?

Well, I think the greatest of all questions *is* answerable. In fact, I think there is a self-writing Script for existence and I think it can be re-engineered and made understandable.

While such bold proclamations may at first blush seem absurd, I think such a view is largely indebted to our traditionally limited ways of looking at how the world, and life, came to be.

In my opinion, the standard explanations for how there came to be the universe are conceptually inadequate. "The Explanation = God" is not an appropriate answer because it leaves out one important bit of information: the explanation for making the architect called "God." [By the way, when I refer to God in this book, I'm not talking about the spiritual entity that most people believe in as a matter of faith. I'm talking about God in a strictly philosophical sense—as the supposed logical foundation for existence.] Also, "The Explanation = An Accident" is not an appropriate answer because it also leaves out one important bit of information: the origin of the eggs that mysteriously got broken (i.e., the empty space, high temperatures, and quantum instability presumed before the The Accident could even happen). This latter scenario, though favored by many modern scientists, is equivalent to providing a Script for starting up the universe from scratch, *albeit while presuming not only eggs, but a Stove for them to fry upon.* Well, how did those eggs and that Stove get there?

Logically speaking, that "Stove" is just as mysterious of a starting point as any presumed God. In fact, I think both presumptions are logically impossible as starting points. Something else must be operating behind the scenes to allow there to be either a God or a Stove. There must be a mechanism of some sort already in place that allows such things to be possible, and my view is that there should be a way to reverse engineer things to determine exactly what that mechanism is/was.

These standard explanations are inadequate because we would just be defining one term (i.e., "the Explanation for a Universe") as being equivalent with other terms (i.e., "God," "Stove"). What we need to understand is how the ingredients of the universe originally came to be, and how they eventually all came together. This requires a different, and I submit *a better*, way of looking at the internal machinery of the universe. Before going on with our story, however, let's take a bit closer of a look at both God and Chance as explanatory devices for our origins.

God Did It!

The scientific community has long considered the concept of God to be an overly-simplistic way of "filling in the gaps" when a better, more comprehensive, answer is not easily forth-coming. Well, I think the scientific derision of a "god of the gaps" is well-founded. Solutions to problems should never have to rely on Magic, and an inexplicable God is equivalent to Magic.

Still, the concept of God is one of the most enduring concepts known to humanity. Most of the assumptions that guided many of the early scientists were founded upon a belief in *rationality* and in *God*. Had scientists not believed in a rational world created by God, it's difficult to believe why anyone would have bothered trying to figure out the universe in the first place. Consider the following assumptions held by most seventeenth-century scientists (of which the great Sir Isaac Newton was but one), as here succinctly described by Kitty Ferguson in *The Fire in the Equations*:

- The universe is *rational*, reflecting both the intellect and the faithfulness of its Creator. It has pattern, symmetry, and predictability to it. Effect follows cause in a dependable manner. For these reasons, it is not futile to try to study the universe.

- The universe is *accessible* to us, not a closed book but one open to our investigation. Minds created in the image of the mind of God can understand the universe God created.

- The universe has *contingency* to it, meaning that things could have been different from the way we find them, and chance and/or choice have played a role in making them what they are. Whether this is contingency in the sense that chance and choice play an on-going role within the universe, or merely in the sense that there was an initial chance occurrence or choice which brought about this universe instead of a different one or none at all, one cannot learn about the universe by pure thought and logic alone. Knowledge comes by observing and testing it.

- There is such a thing as *objective* reality. Because God exists and sees and knows everything, there is a truth behind everything. Reality has a hard edge to it and does not cave in or shift like sands in the desert in response to our opinions, perceptions, preferences, beliefs, or anything else. Reality is not a democracy. There is something definite, some raw material, out there for us to study.

- There is *unity* to the universe. There is an explanation—one God, one equation, or one system of logic—which is fundamental to everything. The universe operates by underlying laws which do not change in an arbitrary fashion from place to place, from minute to minute, or even millennium to millennium. There are no loose ends, no real contradictions. At some deep level, everything fits. (Ferguson, 1994)

Delete the word "God" in this passage and replace it with some variation of the phrase "scientific Law/s" and suddenly these assumptions don't look too far off from what most scientists today take as a given. Belief in a rational, understandable universe is fundamental to science. What's more, this belief was originally vindicated by the assumption of God's existence. Had there been no idea of God, there might not have been a desire to learn of the universe's underlying order. That's because *sans God* why assume an underlying order at all? Well, that's the question that scientists are saddled with today, and that's precisely why you see God's name frequently mentioned in popular science books. While scientists have long since sliced away the "theory of God" from legitimate workaday science, they are still looking for what the idea of God vindicates: the assurance of rationality and order. Hence, the idea of God is still quite important, tied up as it is with many of the assumptions behind the modern sciences (and lest we forget, the sciences have been *very* successful). So then, I don't think the idea of God should be dismissed without an appropriate amount of discussion and acknowledgement.

The most popular "proof" for God's existence is called the ontological argument. St. Anselm, in the eleventh century, was the first to make this argument famous and it was later defended in varying forms by philosophers Leibniz and Descartes. The ontological argument goes as follows:

God is defined as "that (being) than which nothing greater can be conceived." If God existed merely as an idea, then He would not be the greatest conceivable being, for we can easily conceive of a greater who exists not only in mind but also reality, and that being would then be God. Therefore, for God to exist in mind but not reality leads to a logical contradiction—so God must exist both in mind and in reality. The attempt, here, is to show that the proposition "God exists" is analytical—its truth being evident *a priori*. In other words, to understand the notion of the subject *God*, implies that the predicate, *existence*, is contained within that subject. Therefore, *"God" implies God's existence*. (Copleston, 1985)

A pointed refutation of the ontological argument is that it is a product of definitional circularity. So long as you think that the concept of a Perfect Being makes sense, then sure, it simply follows that for that Being to be Perfect it must therefore exist, by definition. However, that's just like saying because I have an idea of a Perfect-Tasting Ham Sandwich, therefore a Perfect-Tasting Ham Sandwich must exist. You see, for that Ham Sandwich to be Perfect-Tasting, it by definition must exist; for how could it be Perfect-tasting if it didn't exist? Obviously, such arguments never get beyond the realm of *defining into existence the very definitions that should be proven.* It needs to be explained why we should assume that the ideas of a "Perfect Being" and a "Perfect-Tasting Ham Sandwich" make sense.

A more subtle difficulty with this argument concerns its inherent assumption that the Law of non-Contradiction should apply. This problem has received little ink, so I'll have to specify what I mean here. Basically, the fundamental claim that the ontological argument makes consists of the following: "for God to exist in mind but not reality leads to a logical contradiction—so God must exist both in mind and in reality." This intrinsically assumes that the Law of non-Contradiction is a metaphysical absolute and that anything violating this Law is an automatic no-no. It's like saying that even if there was no God, somehow the Law of non-Contradiction would nevertheless automatically ensure God's actual existence. This is pretty magical stuff. The Law of non-Contradiction is being presumed to be even more fundamental than God, such that if no Law of non-Contradiction, then there's no possibility for God. Well, how did that Law get there, and why should we even assume that it applies to anything? These questions point to very basic issues that will be returned to later. As of now, however, suffice it to say that nothing should be taken for granted, nothing should be presumed, including the Law of non-Contradiction.

The most intuitively compelling argument in favor of God is probably the Design argument (also known as the teleological argument). Perhaps the most famous Design argument came from William Paley, who used an analogy between natural mechanisms and a watch. Paley maintained that if one were to stumble upon a watch while crossing a heath, then after examining its intricate workings, it would be reasonably concluded that the watch must have been designed for a purpose by an intelligent mind. He thought that the orderly arrangement of the planets in the solar system, the complex organization of living things, and the intricate mechanism of the human eye paid evidence to an intelligent designer, even more so than in the case of the watch. The rich mixture of complexity and order that we find in life sure can seem suspicious

at times (for some people more so than others); as though it all works a little *too* well. Of course, others might look at that same evidence and be impressed at how obvious it is that it's not God behind the strings at all. Nope, so if not God, then it must be Chance…

Chance Did It!

The 16th Century Archbishop James Usher added up all the dates in the Bible and determined that "the world was created on 22nd October, 4004 B.C. at 6 o'clock in the evening." Today, while most cosmologists and astronomers support the theory that there was indeed a starting point—a big bang, a "creation" of sorts—they believe that it happened to have occurred some 15-20 *billion* years ago. Well, although I appreciate the granularity of Usher's declaration, I'm still going to have to side with the scientists on this one.

The traditional big bang theory describes the universe's beginning as a primordial explosion. The explosion did not occur at a particular time and place, as the space-time continuum did not yet exist. However, many people get caught up on the idea that the big bang *must* have taken place at some particular time (first, there was not time, they reason, and then at some distinct point there was time). But there's actually a bit of a paradox here. For example, there's simply no such thing as a "smallest number greater than Ø." Any given "small number" (say 1/1,000,000) can be halved and halved again, indefinitely. The same is true for "time." Any "earliest time" can always be halved and halved again. Accordingly, does it not follow that there can be no "earliest time"?

In any event, the explosion represented a transition from enormous density and temperature to ever decreasing density and temperature as space itself expanded. After the explosion, the universe is said to have been a murky soup of radiant energy and atomic particles. A cooling and thinning out of the universe followed. Finally, we are left today with a universe that is said to be both expanding and facing an uncertain future—big crunch, or heat death?

Two of the leading scientific hypotheses for the big bang incorporate quantum mechanics in their equations and are called *vacuum genesis* and *quantum genesis*. Traditionally, the central problem of cosmogony has always been how to explain something coming from nothing. By "something" is meant our space-time universe of matter and energy. By "nothing" is meant…, well this has always been a bit more problematic. The classical notion was that "nothing" was a vacuum, the empty space between particles of matter. This notion has always been controversial, as witnessed by the historical inquiries into whether empty space must really be filled with a something after all; an ether perhaps? In the modern age of quantum physics, the quantum vacuum is never really empty, possessing turbulent "virtual" particles (some commentators have even suggested that quantum mechanics vindicates the ether theorists from days past). What is a "virtual" particle, you might be asking? Well, let's revisit quantum physics, shall we?

Virtual particles can be thought of as representing the mathematical possibility, as espoused by physicist Heisenberg's indeterminacy principle, of a "real" particle arriving at a given time and place. According to quantum physics, every "real" particle is surrounded by a plethora of virtual particles and antiparticles bubbling up out of the vacuum, interacting with one another in a mutually annihilating manner simply to vanish away entirely. The seething micro-world of the quantum vacuum, from which virtual particles constantly emerge and annihilate, is not merely some dislocated abstraction having little or nothing to do with reality. The quantum world has even been a bona fide practical success in the technologies. The billion-dollar TV industry is a testament to the practical use of turning electron potentialities into not only a highly stable medium but also a very profitable one (and I ask you, where would we be as a society today without *American Idol*?).

The mathematics behind virtual-particle production is intriguingly open-ended in that there's no upper limit on either the masses or the lifetimes of the particles that can pop out of a vacuum. The supposition is that a vacuum with a greater amount of energy—as some suggest would have been the case at the big bang's beginning—might potentially give birth to a particle as massive as a planet. Although such an event would be highly unlikely, it's true enough that it need have happened but once.

But what are we really talking about here? The laws of quantum mechanics indeed allow for the spontaneous appearance of matter from out of nothing (a false vacuum), but only so long as: 1) a corresponding antimatter also appears simultaneously, and 2) the matter and antimatter unite and annihilate each other back into nothing (or the false vacuum) in so short a time that their presence is not even measurable. Given this, it is little wonder that the scenario of a quantum big bang is attractive to many a scientist since it makes the big bang theoretically explainable without requiring a direct cause; as matter is allowed to spontaneously appear. Obviously, however, a universe actually erupting from this annihilation would contradict the central tenet that matter and antimatter must both appear simultaneously and cancel each other out.

Or maybe we have to fudge this tenet to get what we want; because something fluky only needed to happen once, right?

Well, my view is that it's intrinsically *impossible* for a fluky something to happen at such a root-level context. That would require a randomness generator, or a fluke generator, and such an assumption would be untenably question-begging. Does a randomness generator then become a more basic principle than quantum effects? What explains the randomness generator? And, more pointedly, if something else explains the randomness generator, then where does it all stop? This is the familiar dichotomy that has plagued all thoughts about existence; believe in an irrational *endless regress* or believe in an impossible *beginning*?

Here's a profound principle for us to go by: KISS. You've probably heard of it before. It stands for Keep It Simple, Stupid. The "It" in question represents the Script we'll be considering—and it's got to be *very* simple, like any respectable self-writing Script should be.

A central assumption we must always make is one of inertia. An object in motion remains in motion, unless there's some reason why it shouldn't. Likewise, a thing is what it is and its characteristics won't change unless there's some reason to account for that change.

For the sake of argument, let's assume along with the scientific community that the concept of "nothingness" means "false vacuum." Well, a false vacuum according to quantum mechanics is equivalent to saying that its inertial state is self-annihilating, so clearly we're dealing here with the inexplicable and the magical when the inertial state is mysteriously broken. Theoretically, matter and anti-matter should emerge together at the big bang in mutual self-annihilation. Lucky for us, they apparently have yet to meet. Perhaps their union has been delayed for our benefit according to some sort of "Anthropic Principle" (as will be shortly defined). Or perhaps either matter or antimatter was asymmetrically more prevalent than the other. Or perhaps the quantum mechanics at the beginning of things behaved differently than the quantum mechanics of today (in which case, science would no longer have anything of interest to say on the matter, as cosmologists would be left to speculate what quantum mechanics' original behavior might have been like without any empirical evidence for or against their assertions). Any which way you look at it, the asymmetry is an unresolved mystery and the justifications touched upon here have been terribly unsatisfying to say the least.

Suffice it to say that the difficulty of how something came from nothing, or how there came to be something in the first place, has been answered via the modern theory of vacuum genesis by redefining "nothingness" to mean "that which is teeming with quantum activity." An oft-repeated knock against this theory is how linear and ordinary it is in scope. It's a double-edged sword really. The suggestion that known physical laws can extend all the way back to explain the beginnings of the universe seems a bit far-fetched and question-begging. It's question-begging in the same way that explaining how bowling balls are composed of tinier bowling balls all the way down would be question-begging. We haven't "explained" a bowling ball's composition by simply hypothesizing ever smaller bowling balls. We have merely begged the original question involving what a bowling ball is composed of. An appropriate explanation for the composition of bowling balls demands an *other than* rather than a *smaller of the same* and quantum genesis gives us only the latter, not the former. And that should give us pause for thought. But also notice that if a quantum role is not presumed, then there can be no possible scientific answer to the greatest of all puzzles.

Perhaps an even more definitive argument against the theory of vacuum genesis in so far as it's sometimes mistakenly considered a "theory of existence" concerns the already mentioned fact that we're dealing with a theory where the word "vacuum" is defined as meaning "that which is teeming with quantum activity." So then, keeping to that definition it logically follows that from out of a sea of quantum activity there can sprout many a universe (of which ours would be just one in a virtual coat-rack of universes).

How is this different from what we've already seen in another context—defining God as Perfect and then saying that "because God is Perfect, by definition he must therefore exist (since a *non*existent Perfect God would be a contradiction in terms)?" Yes, I agree that so long as we *define* God as "Perfect" or *define* a vacuum as "teeming with quantum activity" then it obviously follows that, *by definition*, God Exists and that, *by definition*, many a universe can sprout. So what? These arguments do not get beyond the level of word-play and superficiality. It still needs to be explained why such definitions should be accepted. After all, up to this point, we have, in effect, done little more than offer an explanation of existence that disingenuously presumes existence all the way down!

The upshot is that vacuum genesis is not a "theory of existence," it's a "theory of the big bang." We will need to go one logical step back in the process of things to have a chance at actually explaining existence.

Before getting too far ahead of ourselves, perhaps we should find some time here to consider a very basic question: How could a vacuum state be responsible

for a universe such as ours that has regular physical laws rather than just some ill-structured "non"-verse of random things just happening?

There are two main answers to this question, and at least the first of them in my opinion is quite persuasive. First, there have been many studies from a number of fields of inquiry that all converge on one finding: that various complex physical laws can seemingly emerge spontaneously from a simple, or even a chaotic state (sound familiar?). Second, sometimes the so-called anthropic principle is used to point out that because we are here at all means that we have to exist in a finely-tuned universe with many built-in rules of operation, otherwise we could not exist. If the universe were truly chaotic, it would be impossible for us to be here marveling at it, so because we are here it must be ordered and structured. That's the so-called anthropic principle. The anthropic principle has been used to support everything from providing evidence for the existence of a "multiverse," providing evidence for the existence of an all-powerful networked robot-God, to providing—in the minds of a brave few—little evidence for much of anything at all. I favor the latter as I regard all of the anthropic cosmological arguments to be as linear in scope as Malthus' dire but false conclusions drawn from considerations of an unchecked population growth and world food supply without properly taking into account technological advances. The world is *not* linear. The variables are constant and come from all sides all at once, and that's why the future is unpredictable.

Turning now to "quantum genesis," the main proponent for this theory has been Stephen Hawking, holder of Newton's old chair as Lucasian Professor of Mathematics at Cambridge University. Understanding that the laws of relativity break down if the big bang is assumed a singularity, Hawking began to explore the prospect of interpreting the origin of the universe in terms of quantum probabilities. In his explorations, Hawking used esoteric tools such as "imaginary time" (a hypothetical time measured in terms of imaginary numbers—like the square root of –1) and Richard Feynman's "sum over histories" (a method of calculating all the possible past trajectories of a particle).

Hawking suggested that space-time was finite but unbounded, using the analogy that the universe diverged from the singularity of genesis like longitude lines proceeding from the North Pole on a globe of the earth: "If the suggestion that space-time is finite but unbounded is correct," Hawking said, "the big bang is rather like the North Pole of the earth. To ask what happens before the big bang is a bit like asking what happens on the surface of the earth one mile north of the North Pole. It's a meaningless question."

A major difficulty with Hawking's "quantum genesis" is his insistence that since the big bang brought space-time along with it, it is therefore meaningless to talk about a "before" to the big bang. Okay, slow down. The space-time introduced by the big bang is the space-time that we know and love and with which we are familiar. The fact that our space-time was nonexistent at the start of the big bang does not negate the possibility, or perhaps I should say the probability, that some sequence or process prior to the big bang must have been responsible for the big bang. Hawking's "imaginary time" begs the question of where the quantum principle came from that all the histories are supposedly following. Basically, while the big bang might not have begun in "our" space-time, sequential movement of any sort would still indicate some form of "time." And this brings up a slew of obvious and repetitive questions: where did quantum mechanics come from? What explains its existence?

To actually explain the existence of quantum mechanics, we need an *other than* not *more of the same*. And so we need to reject the idea of a "self-contained" quantum answer—either of the vacuum or genesis sort—as ultimately nonexplanatory. While either might suffice as a theory of the big bang, neither suffices as a theory of existence.

The universe as explained by quantum chance is as *inexplicable* as trying to explain the liquidness of milk by hypothesizing tiny milk-like objects. The question is entirely begged: How did material things come to be? Well, first there was a material thing…

A more satisfactory model must explain *how* space-time came to exist. As Stephan Hawking himself wrote, "What is it that breathes fire into the equations? Why does the Universe go to all the bother of existing?" The assumption that space-time *always* existed for no better reason than it just always existed (i.e., the quantum vacuum was always out there) lacks coherence. It does not provide an explanation as to the way things actually unfolded in our procedure-based universe.

The Criteria

The problem that both God and Chance share as possible explanations for existence is that they are *inexplicable*. God is inexplicable as a concept because it defies all rational endeavors at attempting to understand its origins. In fact, God supposedly has no origin as it definitionally must exist, eternally. If we regard this concept as a first postulate or a foundational axiom, then our job becomes that much easier in describing how the universe came to be (i.e., "God made it"). However, it's a weak argument to make when it is begun with such a magical assumption. Why and how did God come to be? Why and how does God have the properties that God has?

With the above questions posed, we are now in a position to establish our first criterion: Any First Axiom used to understand the origins of our universe must be *rationally explicable*. What I mean by "rationally explicable" is that the First Axiom, to be acceptable, must be self-defining; it must detail its own necessity. For lack of a better analogy, this can be viewed as equivalent to a built-in program on a computer's motherboard that tells the computer how to start up. In our case, however, we don't have the luxury of logical back-peddling. There's no programmer to fall back upon, as that would entail the same sort of start up program that we were initially attempting to define. The other criteria that this book will be operating under consist of the following:

1. The theory should follow the rules of science (be consistent with and compatible to its findings) *and*:
    a. Be either scientifically verifiable or founded upon a necessary absolute;
    b. Be able to explain and predict both existence and consciousness, at least in theory.

2. The theory should illuminate the ancient mystical conceptions of God, Being, Non-Being, Yin-Yang, Universal Self, and the One and the Many in an ingenious and otherwise non-obvious manner. It must "bridge the gap" between the hard sciences and spirituality. If the many imaginative and mystical conceptions of the Real inspired by spirituality cannot be *accounted for*—only ignored and called illusory—then no legitimate theory has been found.

3. The theory must not beg the question by secretly presuming that which it is trying to argue for in a circular and unhelpful manner. For instance, explaining the solidity of bricks by hypothesizing that small brick-like objects account for the solidity of bricks, does not so much answer the question as beg it. For what, after all, accounts for that brick-like solidity? Likewise, it's improper and unhelpful to presume that existence has always existed, for example, due to tiny "existence-like" particles (i.e., a "quantum vacuum"). Some sort of

other than process must be articulated that can indirectly account for the obviousness of that which is before us.

4.   Everything can be reverse engineered: meaning that there's a process and a mechanics—a way things work—behind anything and everything. Anything and everything must be held accountable to a process that makes it come to be. This blanket statement is all-encompassing and has absolutely no exceptions.

To conclude, then, I think that the terms God and Chance (as defined) are logically identical in that they both rely on first axioms that are inexplicable, and so fail to meet my criteria to be adequate theories of existence. In my view, an appropriate first axiom must write itself, it must self-describe its own workability. Hence, our reverse engineering project is only just beginning…

BYTE THREE:

THE THEME

http://www.philscanlan.net/

The "First Cause"

Author Howard Bloom in his thought-provoking book *Global Brain* provides his rendition of the standard explanation for how there came to be anything:

> Roughly 12 billion years ago, a submicroscopic pinpoint of false vacuum arose in the nothingness and expanded at a rate beyond human comprehension, doubling every 10-34 seconds.

The upshot is that we have a description here for *how the big bang occurred*, but not an explanation for *how there is anything at all*. What does it really mean to say that the universe erupted from out of a false vacuum?

Basically, I think this description causes confusion. The confusion lies with "a theory of the big bang" and "a theory of existence" and those are simply two distinct things. Even assuming that scientific interpretations about the early stages of our universe are correct, and that we grant there was indeed a false vacuum from which a big bang erupted, we are still left with this absolutely meaningless and inexplicable idea of a "false vacuum." Where did that come from? What magical Rule-Book of Creation accounts for its arising? Without further explanation, I find this conception in so far as it is a theory of existence to be unconvincing.

The human mind understands things best by use of analogy and story-telling. For this book's central insight to truly resonate, an appropriate context is needed. Without the appropriate context, the reader cannot hope to have an "a-ha" experience. I sincerely hope that I have offered that context for you up to this point—in a linear and understandable way (the big, bad world might be non-linear, but we sure like things to be as linear as possible!).

The central insight of this book consists of providing an accountability for existence. I assume a "principle of sufficient reason" such that an accountability for what might otherwise be considered *the unaccountable* (or *the inexplicable*) is pre-supposed. Perhaps a little discussion is appropriate.

There has been much philosophical discussion through the ages about how if anything began to exist without a cause, then it would in effect have caused itself. This is acknowledged to be impossible since for something to have caused itself it would have had to exist before itself. Another form of argument suggests that if a thing came into existence without a cause, then it would in effect be caused by nothing, and nothing cannot be the cause of anything. Both lines of reasoning presuppose the notion that something must "cause" something else. Even if it's claimed there is no cause for a thing, it's still being assumed that the thing in question must have caused itself or that literally "nothing" must have somehow been the cause. Talk about linguistic confusion!

Despite these age-old conundrums, and the fact that the 18th century philosopher David Hume was undoubtedly correct in suggesting that a "necessary connection" will never be identifiable between a supposed effect and its cause, I nonetheless believe that accountability for existence should be presupposed.

A counter-argument to my presumption might suggest that since quantum mechanics does not require standard cause-effect relationships (as it allows for the spontaneous appearance and disappearance of quantum particles), then quantum behavior must be considered an example of a scientific theory without accountability. Therefore, accountability should not be presumed as a characteristic of existence. The scientific theory of quantum mechanics is, however, highly accountable for itself, in this case offering a generally well accepted set of mathematics for its explanation. The principles and rules that embody quantum mechanics, allowing for the possibility of non-causal events, are being offered as the explanation, the cause, the what's accountable, for quantum behavior. Quantum behavior is thus hardly an example of unaccountability. Quite the opposite!

We have seen that the ancient dilemma of a first cause (God or Chance?) has not been successfully side-stepped by quantum mechanics and modern theorizing. Many in the scientific community, including Hawking himself, recognize that the principles and rules of quantum mechanics logically demand an explanation, an accountability of some sort. Scientists are not overtly interested in these concerns, as they do not express a supposition amenable to the scientific method of proof. Scientists are much more prone, and for good reason, to limit their scope to explaining phenomena that are directly observable.

Sir Arthur Stanley Eddington made the following wonderful analogy:

> Let us suppose that an ichthyologist is exploring the life of the ocean. He casts a net into the water and brings up a fishy assortment. Surveying his catch, he preceeds in the usual manner of a scientist to systematize what it reveals. He arrives at two generalizations:
>
> (1) No sea-creature is less than two inches long.
> (2) All sea-creatures have gills.

In applying this analogy, the catch stands for the body of knowledge which constitutes physical science, and the net for the sensory and intellectual equipment which we use in obtaining it. The casting of the net corresponds to observations.

An onlooker may object that the first generalization is wrong. "there are plenty of sea-creatures under two inches long, only your net is not adapted to catch them." The ichthyologist dismisses this objection contemptuously. "Anything uncatchable by my net is ipso facto outside the scope of ichthyological knowledge, and is not part of the kingdom of fishes which has been defined as ichthyological knowledge. In short, what my net can't catch isn't fish." (1958, p.16)

Likewise, the knee-jerk response has been, "if science can't study it, then it's meaningless." Such a response is both bad science and bad philosophy. The only thing that logically follows is that there might be truths that exist outside of science's methodology. Whether or not we can ever actually get to those truths (with or without the use of scientific principles) remains an open question.

At this point, it may seem that the acceptance of some sequence or process occurring outside of our known space-time, and therefore outside of what science can investigate, implies that we are really just backing up the initial problem of a first cause one step, not actually offering a better overall explanation. In this regard, one might reasonably ask "what explains the sequence or process that supposedly explains the big bang?"

Well, I've asked that question myself. And it seems absolutely fundamental that the explanation, the accountability, we are looking for is at a Buck Stops Here level. The sequence or process must be self-defining. It must be a sequence or process that boot-straps itself into existence.

My goal is to convey to you what that "boot-strapping Script" must be like, as it ultimately explains (even if only indirectly) the introduction of the big bang. In my opinion, everything has some sort of explanation. We live in a world where science works, where, for instance, our planet Earth rotates around the sun in a regular and predictable manner. What this suggests to me is that there is a computational chain of events that can be traced from Now all the way back to the beginning of things, to a Buck Stops Here—such that a necessarily existing boot-strapping Script must ultimately account for the explanation of the big bang.

"Ouch!," some might be saying. "Aren't you just arguing backwards to get what you want?" You must understand that the explanation for existence pretty much has to be simple yet comprehensive. Also, whatever the explanation for the big bang might be, it cannot be a one-shot deal, as it needs to incorporate the very real possibility that "our" big bang is just one among many. And if we look at it expansively like that, whereby big bangs have been happening long since forever, then we are forced to realize that whatever the explanation for existence might be it had best be *necessary* and *eternal*. And this is where my necessarily existing self-writing Script enters.

Some might be wondering why I call this hypothetical boot-strapping Script "necessarily existing." Perhaps to some it may even seem that I've just taken a leap in logic here. After all, how does one get "a necessarily existing boot-strapping Script" from the unoriginal presumption that everything needs to be held accountable and that all things have an explanation? Well, this really cannot be otherwise. We are talking about a process at a contextual stage so deep that to call this process "boot-strapping" is definitionally the same as calling it "necessarily existing." There must be some quality that this process has that makes it boot-strap, and this must perpetually be the case. Since nothing else exists at this fundamental contextual level to impede it, the boot-strapping Script must therefore necessarily exist.

The reasons that can be given for why this boot-strapping Script has to "necessarily exist" is part of a long tradition that in antiquity would have typically been equated with God. Although I might not agree with that conclusion, nevertheless I believe that any sort of Buck Stops Here implies a situation where causality breaks down, and necessity reigns.

Before consenting to any of this, the reader should be made aware that there are plenty of people who would be skeptical about my project as thus far articulated. For example, a logical positivist like the late Alfred Ayer might have taken exception to my project of deducing knowledge about the nature of existence through "first principles." Logical positivism was quite influential in the early part of the 20th century. It was a system of thought that required statements to have formal rules. A statement was to be classified as either (a) analytic—logically true or false, (b) empirically testable, or if neither (a) nor (b) it was to be classified as (c) nonsense, a pseudo-statement. All untestable statements were to be considered nonsense. Such formalism and structure still has great appeal for many people today. It seems tight—well defined. Unfortunately, it is *too* tight: self-refutingly too tight. The criterion *the meaning of a sentence is its method of verification* is neither analytically true, nor testable. That leaves "nonsense," according to its own criteria.

Turns out that logical positivism is a weak comfort—a security blanket for those who won't accept the world as it is (very *messy*). Nevertheless, a logical positivist like Ayer would not like anything that smacks of metaphysics, and a rationally-divined *a priori* truth called a "boot-strapping process" can easily be construed as trying to deduce the entire world from a mere tautology; i.e., speculative metaphysics. I absolutely respect that aspect of logical positivism. There's too much speculative nonsense in the world. Even if logical positivism in toto does not provide a satisfying view, surely we can all agree that it yet possesses some good, reasonable positions—its dismissal of speculative metaphysics being one of them.

So what's my response to the claim that only other tautologies can be deduced from a tautology? That my project is Dead On Arrival?

My "boot-strapping process" is indeed a first principle, an *a priori* truth, a tautology, an ultimately irrational axiom (*axioms really are ultimately irrational*). But it's also inherently paradoxical; contradictory. I define a paradox to be a "true contradiction"—and *literally* anything and everything can be derived from a contradiction. To say the least, these are *very* powerful concepts. This fact plays an important role in my necessarily existing first principle. [Consider some of the paradoxical features of quantum mechanics as previously discussed. Consider also as previously discussed the central paradox that Gödel demonstrated—forever limiting all of formal mathematics to an incompletable system.]

The theory of a boot-strapping Script presented in this book remains the central feature of my viewpoint. The rest of my worldview interpretation is admittedly warmed-over computationalism and Darwinian natural-selectionism. This latter part of my worldview suggests that the universe can be likened to a giant algorithm, one that at its base varies a theme (much like natural selection is a natural process that varies the theme of an organism's genes and DNA).

In some respects, this computationalist worldview is traditionalist in that the idea of having a "theme" and "variations" on a theme can be likened to a "One" and a "Many," two concepts having a particularly long and troubled history in the school of speculative hard-knocks. The main difference with my interpretation is that the "theme" I propose is not assumed to be some sort of transcendent One having no relationship to our world. I rather interpret the theme to already contain at least some complexity in that it's a boot-strapping Script. Likewise, although my theory requires that this Script take place prior

to our known space-time, this by itself does not imply that it's an utterly transcendent entity, no more so than a boot-device is transcendent to a computer. Granted, there might be some terminology difficulties with this analogy, but the point remains that there is a link; a procedural connection.

Continuing on with the computer analogy, the Script I'm discussing can be likened to a computer program that's responsible for boot-strapping existence to get to the conditions needed for a "big bang" (or, quite frankly, whatever theory science has available evidence to support). Given the terminology that I'm using, it should be obvious that this Script does not consist of the material stuff of our space-time universe. The underlying laws of physics cannot be a part of this Script, nor can any physical laws in the usual sense (let alone any complicated mathematics). Rather, what the Script must deal with is a sort of foundational logic brought about by brute necessity. This necessity is similar to the modern Einsteinian conception of a gravity that is nothing more than the after-effects of a curvature in space-time brought about by large mass structures. The curvature of space-time cannot help but result in the phenomenon of gravity. Likewise, the Script cannot help but "run" due to certain foundational, logical structures.

I believe the foundational logic to be composed of none other than the primordial dichotomy between "existing" and "not existing" and the unsolvable dilemma that ensues when we assume that there can be no assumptions. If we assume that there are no initial inclinations or favorings, then we are led to the conclusion, as I will be detailing shortly, that a self-booting script arises forming a devastating conflict. Basically, using standard English to relate the underlying logic involved, the script reads something like the following:

Should there be?
Should there not be?
Should there be?
Should there not be?

There are other ways of expressing the idea involved. And technically, I'm cheating by using the categorical buckets of "be" and "not be." The conflict between opposites is what's key. Relative to the Script itself, the opposites are as yet undefined (the Script doesn't "know" that it's debating between existence and nonexistence—they just happen to be two equally plausible potentialities that happen to be utterly contradictory to one another). Nonetheless, I think the fundamental nature of the Script is represented well enough and pointedly enough by the questions asked above. And note this: those questions, relative to the Script itself, are unanswerable! I'm suggesting that those questions are "asked" to begin with because the foundational logic is such that the Script cannot help but ask them. The potentialities are equally plausible—*either* some fragile possibility exists, *or* not even that—and they're mutually exclusive, they cannot both be the case at one and the same time.

Relative to the Script itself, understand that we cannot assume that the universe should favor an "on" position over an "off" position—or a "fragile possibility" over "not even that." The favoring for "on" must be incorporated in the explanation, not vice-versa! We are dealing with a "script" at such a deep-level context that it doesn't even know whether it should be in an "on" position or an "off" position, let alone have any rules or guidelines telling it what "on" or "off" *means*.

I understand that when I say "we are dealing with a Script," it can be disingenuously argued that I'm assuming a something, a system, that cannot decide between an off position and an on position. This is really not true. The deep-level script we're talking about is entirely and only the indeterminate conflict of whether or not there should be a fragile possibility or not even that. There is nothing more to it. The Script does not exist prior to the conflict, it's not stored in a Magic Book somewhere, rather the Script *is* the conflict.

Now the important thing to note here is that provided the assumption of no assumptions is correct, the conclusion becomes self-evident. There will either be a 1 or there will be a Ø, but by definition of the concepts involved, there cannot be both. Although, and this is a subtle distinction that is very important, there's no Rule in the Script that says there cannot be both.

Always operate by the following maxim: if it's not in the Script, then it don't exist (to vary a well-known phrase about glove-fitting and acquitting). And all the Script amounts to is that of a conflict between 1 and Ø. [While on the subject of interpreting the Script, the reader should note that as much as possible, I'll be taking the perspective of the Script and how that Script must behave, so just be prepared for that.]

So, to summarize, we get this metaphorical Script that has no way of answering itself because it's a paradox—the Law of non-Contradiction *both* applies *and* does not apply at one and the same time. This is a conflict ripe for an Illegal Operation error message. Where's the instruction manual? Where's the technical support?

Before further demonstrating this book's sole original insight, let's review some basic logical concepts:

The law of excluded middle:
"P is true, or not-p is true."

The law of non-Contradiction:
"It is not true that p and not-p are both true."

A statement of relation:
"'a exists' is equivalent to 'x exists and x is a.'"

Believe it or not, the theory of existence presented in this book exists at such a conceptually simple context that the above logical definitions are all that will be needed. And so, from such simple rules a complex and rich structure will emerge (hey, does that sound familiar?). And, quite frankly, it had better be this simple—because if it was any more complicated we would have every right to be deeply suspicious of smuggled-in assumptions!

Before I follow through with the presentation of my theory, however, there is something I should remind you of: *Our logic is suspect.* Consider some well-known tautologies as they might appear in ordinary-language:

Law of non-Contradiction:	You can't be both happy and sad.
Law of excluded middle:	You either believe in logic or you don't.
DeMorgan's laws:	If a sentence is neither true nor false, then it's both false and true. If nobody's both male and female, then everyone's female or male.
Reductio ad absurdum:	If the world didn't exist, then this sentence wouldn't exist, but clearly this sentence does exist. Therefore the world exists.

One striking thing about these examples is that they don't all seem entirely true or sensible, let alone *satisfying*. The basic problem is that our language is not based on solidly true-or-false concepts. We may hope, though, that our reality is based on some underlying atomic properties that obey logical principles such as the law of non-Contradiction. But remember, more likely than not, our artificial logic will never mesh nicely with our messy world.

Well, allow me to introduce my little theory...

I ask that regardless of what your pet theory may be as to how the universe came to exist, let's agree that the universe must have derived from a state in which all possibilities were equivalent, and where no inclination or preference was favored over any other. And logically, albeit perhaps not intuitively, this assumption also encompasses the idea that *anythingness* could not have been initially preferred over its opposite of *not anythingness*, (or, in my terminology, *the possibility of a possibility* can not have been initially favored over *not even that*). This can be called the "egalitarian approach." Denying this assumption leads to the obvious question about how it could be possible at this stage for a favorite since we're at a level of inquiry prior to the development of working laws and rules capable of favoring one thing over the other (thus breaking the inertial state). And, as I touched upon already, that precludes any probability programs or randomness generators.

Note however, that I cannot prove that the egalitarian approach must be accepted. It's an axiom. An intuitive hunch. But it remains my beginning assumption, and everything else logically follows from that initial assumption. You can quibble about it, but the alternative—the "inegalitarian approach"—seems far more arbitrary and far more question-begging. To my mind, such an approach demands a pre-existing randomness generator. For how else can either on or off be selected? And a theory about existence, operating at this basic-level of a context, simply cannot afford to smuggle in assumptions of that magnitude.

Remember: KISS (Keep It Simple Stupid). Our beginning assumption will be of an ambivalent, inertial state where 1 has no more legitimate right to the throne than does ∅. And so from this assumed perfect symmetry we begin...

Script Abstract:

Axiom:

The *possibility of a possibility* (1) and *not even that* (∅) are contradictory potentials representing the most basic distinction possible, neither having preference over the other.

[Brief Interlude: Note that the very use of "∅" is an obvious contradiction in terms. The symbol "∅" is being used to denote an absence, a nothingness, a not-even-that. Such problems in terminology should not be considered significant.

We are evolutionary products that have derived from out of the 1 position. So our logic should only be expected to apply to 1, not Ø. We're only familiar with 1. Our survival is dependent upon such familiarity. Our survival in no way is dependent upon Ø, so why should our words be expected to describe such a thing in a non-contradictory manner? Why should our minds be expected to truly grasp what utter nothingness implies? If Ø was the state of things there would be no "state of things" to talk about. Nuff said.]

Definitions:

The Law of non-Contradiction states "*x* and *not-x* cannot both be true at the same time." [Note: This is a *human* law and not a *metaphysical* law.]

A **Cosmic Eraser** is a hypothetical device that erases everything in the universe including itself, forcing an indeterminate state in which potentiality both exists and does not exist. Now what happens?

Code:

If the Law of non-Contradiction no longer applies at the point in time where the Cosmic Eraser erases the last remnant of itself, then *possibly*

$$[1 \text{ and } Ø]$$

If the Law of non-Contradiction applies at the point in time where the Cosmic Eraser erases the last remnant of itself, then 1 and Ø are mutually exclusive by definition. Accordingly,

$$[1 \text{ or } Ø]$$

It is **intrinsically indeterminate** whether or not the Law of non-Contradiction applies when the Cosmic Eraser is erased. While the concepts involved are in fact contradictory, there is no metaphysical law established at this point that would render a contradiction *impossible*. At the same time, there is equally no metaphysical law established at this point suggesting that a contradiction should be *possible*. So, the Script doesn't know how to handle the situation

...and/or...

Therefore, [1 & ∅] **and/or** [1 or ∅] represents *the range of logical possibility* between existence and non-existence. **Paradoxically,** the Law of non-Contradiction *both* applies and does not apply after the erasing of the Cosmic Eraser.

The equation is thus; [1 & ∅] **&/OR** [1 or ∅]

I believe this represents a dynamic conflict of existential proportions. This state has got to be unstable, has got to be potentially explosive. Something's just got to give!

Note that I'm using *deductive reasoning* to reach the conclusion of [1 & ∅] **&/OR** [1 or ∅]. After all, I'm making the following logical argument:

Given that

I) 1, ∅ represents the most basic distinction possible, residing at a level prior to any possible preconceived Standards (including the operationality of the Law of non-Contradiction) and that
  i)   neither 1 nor ∅ can be regarded as favored over the other, and that
  ii) there are no other considerations that can be arbitrarily introduced,

*it **necessarily** follows that*

II) [1 and ∅] **AND/OR** [1 or ∅] results.

Note also that this conclusion is *definitional*. Provided that the premises are true, the conclusion must follow. What this demonstrates is that assuming an initial state of inertia (a state in which ∅ is as likely a possibility as 1), we get dilemma. How did the universe ever turn itself on anyway? How could "on" as opposed to the far simpler "off" have ever been chosen?

Let's think about this a bit. Say you have no real quarrel with the way I'm putting words together so far. Deep down, however, you feel that this script-idea is ultimately limited, and for obvious reasons. What makes it run? What breathes fire into it? What makes it executable?

Oh, how glad I am that you asked this!

This particular script is unabashedly executable. At its core, the script deals with contradiction and conflict. A thing cannot both exist and not exist at one

and the same time. This script unwittingly attempts to make just that happen. The result is the only sort of resolution possible: it blows up.

Consider the scenario with different words: Say that "on" is a 1 position and "off" is a Ø position. Importantly, 1 and Ø are utterly contradictory. A 1 position implies a possibility of a possibility, a chance happening, a fluke random occurrence. In short, it implies a spark. As long as there is a possibility of a spark, the spark will eventually happen. What would stop it? A Ø position, on the other hand, is absence. Nothing can only come from nothing. A chance event is impossible in such a (non)state. I've just described the most fundamental opposition possible. The root opposition.

The problem: There's no better reason for there to be 1 as opposed to Ø, or Ø as opposed to 1.

Instantaneously, I believe something on the order of the following must happen:

Since there are no Rules in place (no start-up manual to refer to), and since there's no better reason for there to be 1 as opposed to Ø, there's an instant conflict. Both 1 **and** Ø cannot be the case at once, yet either 1 **or** Ø are equally acceptable alternatives.

1 AND/OR Ø

Devastating Conflict. This is an impossible situation. 1 and Ø cannot both be the case at the same time. Yet either 1 or Ø are equally acceptable alternatives. *What gives?*

Material View: An explosion or spark occurs, thus justifying existence. Simply put, 1 AND/OR Ø is an impossible contradiction. A contradiction that nevertheless happens to be true (a paradox). It does what any self-respecting contradiction would do: it blows up.

Validation View: The conflict is resolved by a validation process such that the metaphorical equivalent of an "I AM" is produced. After all, the conflict of 1 AND/OR Ø is certainly not Ø. It's a pressing conflict (a far cry from absence). Since 1 and Ø cannot both be the case at the same time, and since the conflict demands resolution, a self-referential calculation is performed such that since 1 AND/OR Ø does not equal Ø, therefore 1 AND/OR Ø must equal 1. Therefore, 1. Or, therefore explosion or spark. (Perhaps there's ultimately no interesting difference between 1 and an explosion or spark.) Because this calculation is in some respect self-referential, it is being classified as a primordial form of unconscious-experience.

The Two Views:

These two views may seem very similar. They both seem to get us to the needed Spark that would initiate the big bang, but they are actually quite different and certainly have huge implications for humanity and for what they imply about our place in the greater scheme of things.

If the Material View is true, then some form of awareness and consciousness *is not* an essential ingredient of reality. Reality "exists" regardless of whether or not it's perceived. Our consciousness is literally inexplicable (an evolutionary by-product of chance events). This line of thinking is very compelling in its simplicity.

If the Validation View is true, then some form of unconscious-experience *is* an essential ingredient of reality. Reality only "exists" when it's "experienced" (or validated). To some extent, our experienced universe might rightly be considered a put-up job: a mindless display of Varying a Theme. The Theme in question possesses a fusion of existence/experience, so any possible Variation would have to include existence/experience in some form as well. The contention is that for something to exist, there must be at minimum a self-Validation (an experience, even if only an unconscious experience) of that existence. Otherwise, *according to what* would there be existence? This view appeals to the deeply intuitionist position that any kind of existence/reality demands some kind of corresponding experience and that neither in isolation has any significance or meaning without the other.

Ultimately, I believe the Validation line of thinking to be more compelling than the Material. After all, does the concept of "existence" really have any inherent significance or meaning to it? There's no Universal Dictionary that defines it, or its corollary "non-existence." Both concepts, recall, are only notable relative to the Script in that they are exactly opposite to each other. The only way to build up definitions "on the fly," so to speak, would be by posing one in relation to the other. Relative to each other, one contains an absence and the other a potential. But even from this, we just get opposition followed by a potential contradiction—not anything that denotes "an existing thing." According to this way of thinking, how can 1 be the answer when 1 has yet to be defined? And if 1 is not defined, how can it ever hope to bring about the

concreteness of existing particulars? At least the self-Validation step seems to define 1 for us, allowing a way for 1 to harden and set.

In truth, I'm not sure whether the Material View or the Validation View is correct, as no one can be. I prefer the Validation View, but primarily due to an emotionalist, intuitionist hunch. The Material View is still very possible, and may in actuality be the more elegant solution. By the way, this conundrum is ageless. If a tree falls in the forest and nobody is around, does it really make a sound? Define your terms and then argue until the end of time for those definitions. You'll never get any definitive answer. For this book I adopt the Validation View.

So from this logical foundation, whereupon a necessary contradiction either blows up or becomes self-Validated (and then blows up), we eventually get to the sprawling mess of our daily reality. Notice that the current argument being proposed does not depend on any preordained law, as what's being described is, if anything, a self-writing law. Recall how many a scientist has gotten stuck when attempting to explain the big bang by way of the quantum law and then having no way of explaining the quantum law. As an alternative, I'm presenting a naturalistic and plausible scenario that demonstrates the how's and why's of things as they self-develop. By the way, I want my interpretation of the Script to be thought of as open-source material; to be shared and updated freely. GO!

BYTE FOUR:
CRITICISMS & COMPARISONS

http://www.philscanlan.net/

A Variation on a Theme

My worldview, A Variation on a Theme, is really almost an aside; a conglomeration of computationalism and Darwinian natural selectionism.

Nevertheless, A Variation on a Theme remains my interpretive worldview and since it is my worldview, I would be amiss not to share it. A Variation on a Theme suggests that every single thing within the universe is a product of a shared origin. It also suggests that while distinctions and differences exist in the world, there yet remain commonalities in even the most seemingly disparate of things. It suggests that while there may be many possible universes, all such universes are forced to mimic the template of creation (the original Theme).

Many authors have used broad interpretive strokes to model the world. These strokes may be called systems, networks, cellular automata, complexity, chaos, or any number of other buzz-phrases. In years past, it used to be earth, wind, fire, water, and atoms. I truly believe that attempting to interpret the world in one stroke will forever be an arbitrary project closely associated with personal opinion. It's a sort of poetry, a sort of appreciation.

It's the nature of the world we live in—as it's the ultimate Rorschach test—that it has many qualities that can be interpreted in many different ways.

Why should natural selection have been able to produce human-like consciousness? The implausibility of this seems apparent given the level of order and complexity that is demanded to make it happen. Keep in mind, however, that it's logically impossible for us as organisms to exemplify any characteristic that the universe does not already allow.

It would be nice to plug "consciousness" into the machinery of a worldview, and have it come back with meaningful results—at least relative to that worldview!

And that's the point. We like it when things have meaning. We like possessing an interpretive framework capable of explaining the cosmos in a nutshell—even if the worldview amounts to little more than personal opinion. And so, with much fanfare, I'll now let it fly…

According to my theory of A Variation on a Theme, for any universe to be complex and sustainable it must be the type of universe that can contain life and consciousness, in some form. [Note that this supposition is by no means provable.]

To begin, let's say that The Script describes a sort of eternal conflict/computation *that cannot not be.* There's nothing *mystical* about this: *it cannot possibly be otherwise.* Furthermore, let's say that this Script describes a Buck Stops Here sort of process that can function, for all intents and purposes, as the Mechanism *behind* the mechanisms (with no further *meta*-Mechanism *needed*, or even *possible*). In other words, once in motion it's the Theme. Our particular universe, then, can be regarded as a Variation in a *nonlinear explosion of Variations* upon that Theme, such that every possibility of every single quantum event is explored in the Fullness of That Which Is (this is a variation on the physicist Alan Guth's theory of an Inflationary universe).

Consider what's being said here. Since the Theme is all there is, it is the only thing that can be Varied—anything else would be impossible. An example of this, I believe, is *our* universe. This is natural selection on a Universe of Universes scale. The Many Variations cannot help but follow the constraints of the Theme, for the same reasons that a chicken will never give birth to a cow. Hence, I view our universe as nothing more than an algorithm that was compelled to produce experience as we know it at some point during its computation (understand it's not the universe that becomes aware, but organisms within it), just like in Einstein's conception of a curved space-time a straight-line *cannot help but be curved* because space-time itself is curved. It's not teleological. It's damn near mechanical.

This Variation on a Theme idea is quite intrinsic to Reality. And, as should be expected, we also see Variations on this "Variations on a Theme" Theme crop up all over the place. We see it with DNA and the process of natural selection. We see it, inversely, with human intelligence—a process that allows seemingly disparate Variations to be compressed into singular Themes. Also think of creativity, which, in general (whether a product of human creativity or nature's creativity), seems to boil down to a process that takes a given Theme and tweak-Varies it into many different Variations.

Natural selection does not explain life. Natural selection is a process that happens by default, nonintentionally, to life. So too, A Variation on a Theme is a default process that happens to both organic as well as inorganic structures. Natural selection is not so much a subset of A Variation on a Theme as A Variation on a Theme is a logical extension of the central idea presented in Darwin's theory of natural selection. For instance, the formation of galaxies is an inorganic process, a process that works by default. It's not orthodox natural selection that explains it, but rather an extension of the idea behind natural selection. A Variation on a Theme is not and cannot be a specific example of anything, but rather is a more general term that blankets all processes, both organic and inorganic.

The simple idea of having a Theme, and Varying that Theme constantly and recursively, runs deep and is very powerful. As an example, if DNA could be *perfectly replicated* each and every time, then an organism's chances for survival would decrease if and when environmental conditions change for the worse. An organism's best bet would be to replicate *near-perfectly* every single time (as the current version of DNA is what has proven to be successful in the past), but still have a certain degree of flexibility through random variation. Accordingly, *just in case* things were to drastically change, the organism is not straight-jacketed and doomed to perish: a possibility remains for the organism to happen upon a variation that ensures survival. Notice, however, that the organism has nothing to do with this "strategy." This is the sort of TIT-FOR-TAT strategy that is *forced to happen* in nature, by default: Why? *Because it works.* [Those not possessing this strategy die out over time.]

Another interesting aside here is the explanation for both experience and time provided by the framework of A Variation on a Theme. I think it's a meaningless truism that "the world is my representation" and that a person cannot directly know what a sun or an earth is, but only the presentation that our human senses have of such things. However, our human senses are a product of evolution and do not exist apart from the world, but have rather been formed cumulatively over time by multiple recursive interactions with the world: humans being a patched-together Variation on a Theme, and time simply being the recursive, algorithmic steps that our universe keeps churning through (but more on that later!).

You might be asking: Is there really a need for such a broad interpretation?

Legitimate question. And the answer is by no means decisive but I think it's affirmative. After all, a unifying principle is provided such that everything Varies off a Theme. Such a principle is simple and intuitive, and there's a very good chance that it's true, even if only as a gross approximation.

In a broad, generalized interpretive worldview like A Variation on a Theme, the case can be made that a net is being used that tries to catch all the fish in the ocean. Well, if we get abstract enough, what better net is there then the net of the ocean in its entirety. All fish are in the ocean, and if we define the ocean as being a net, then we have in effect caught all fish with one net. In the same way, the entire universe can be redefined as "material" or "ideal" or "computational," but such abstract terms do not an impressive theory make. It's interpretational. It's poetical. There's no such thing as a perfect worldview. Obviously, I don't put much

intellectual significance in such broad interpretive games. Nonetheless, such a worldview yet provides an emotionally pleasing framework for our minds. Hey, we're only human!

Does the Script's Reasoning Hold Up?

Let's refresh our memories by considering the logical argument for the Script once again:

Given that

I)   a) 1, Ø represents the most basic distinction possible, residing at a level prior to any possible preconceived Standards (including the operationality of the Law of non-Contradiction) and that
b) neither 1 nor Ø can be regarded as favored over the other, and that
c) there are no other considerations that can be arbitrarily introduced,

it necessarily follows that

II)   [1 and Ø] **AND/OR** [1 or Ø] results.

Of the above, the only premise really available to attack would be the first of these, that "1, Ø represents the most basic distinction possible." After all, b) is implied by a) such that provided a) is true, then b) must also be true. For example, given a), how could either 1 or Ø be favored over the other without there being some sort of pre-existing Standard in place to tip the scales one way or the other? And obviously, any such Standard would fall under the category of *possibility of a possibility* and would therefore violate the premise that 1, Ø is the most basic distinction possible. What's true for b) is also true for c). After all, if we accept a), then we are accepting a distinction that is absolute. Provided that we accept the distinction, it's definitionally impossible to introduce any other factors, as all other possible factors (like the Law of non-Contradiction) would already fall under the category of a *possibility of a possibility*. Hence, c) is also implied by a).

Accordingly, to attack the premise, one is forced to take at least a variation of one of the following positions concerning the Cosmic Eraser erasing itself after everything else has already been erased:

1) the erasing of the Cosmic Eraser will lead to nothingness,
2) the erasing of the Cosmic Eraser will still leave a potentiality,
3) the whole idea of a Cosmic Eraser is pure nonsense.

The problems with 1) and 2) should be readily apparent for anybody who has read this far into the book. Proponents of both 1) and 2) would be making metaphysical claims that are founded upon unsupportable presumptions. A proponent of 1) is assuming that the Law of non-Contradiction is some sort of Platonic absolute such that even though *everything has been erased* somehow there's still this mysterious Law of non-Contradiction hanging around. For how else could it be concluded that, "Well, if everything else is already gone and now even this last bit of Cosmic Eraser is also erased, that must leave absolutely nothing." My question would be if there's really *nothing else*, then how did there get to be a Rule such that "If no 1, then ∅"? How is such a Rule even possible at this point? My point is that you'd need such a mysterious Rule to keep *possibility of a possibility* out of the equation.

Concerning position 2), a metaphysical claim is being made that existence is a necessity and that nonexistence is a foregone impossibility. This view might assume that there simply will always be at least a quantum vacuum of potentiality (or a negative energy, or an infinite singularity, or a zero-state entropy, or a conservation of energy, or a...). Granted, this may well be the case—just as it may well be the case that there is a necessarily existing God. However, such claims still need to show how and why such things are even possibly necessary at all. We need accountability!

So then, that leaves us with 3). This option might seem the most promising since the whole notion of a Cosmic Eraser is hypothetical anyway. However, just because a thought experiment can never be empirically verified does not mean that it's nonsensical. After all, a person could never report back that he or she had inadvertently entered a black hole and had consequently been ripped to shreds. Such things are definitional: if what we know about black holes are true, then it's simply impossible to ever enter a black hole and live to talk about it. Likewise it's impossible to ever empirically verify the origins of life, let alone the big bang—based upon the very definitions of these concepts. Perhaps *simulations* could be verified, but obviously not the originals.

A similar thing is going on with the Cosmic Eraser. We can know with certainty that if anything even remotely similar to a Cosmic Eraser erasing itself occurred, then it would be impossible to empirically verify that this happened. Since I regard the concept of a Cosmic Eraser as being possibly equivalent in meaning to the concept of a Big Crunch (depending, of course, on what it turns out that a Big Crunch is really like—and if there will ever even turn out to be such a thing!), my question remains the same whether we choose to dress it up with scientific terminology or not: what happens when the last bit of x disappears (collapses upon itself)? Will there still exist a remainder of some sort? Cosmic Eraser fragments perhaps? Negative energy maybe? An infinite singularity? Or, will there simply be nothingness?

In short, I think that the Cosmic Eraser thought experiment has to be taken on its own terms. Anything less would be intellectually arbitrary (unless, that is, one is really willing to hold that *everything* lacking direct empirical verification is meaningless—including black holes, the big bang, the origins of life, and—egad—even the theory of evolution).

The fact is that we live in a largely ambiguous world and that many of its characteristics are not amenable to direct empirical verification. So, to compensate, we have to make do. For the theory of evolution, we make do with all sorts of supporting indirect evidence (including fossil records and similarities between species and so on), but we still don't have the direct evidence of one species, right now, changing wholesale into another species. For the Script of Existence, we make do with an analytical necessity.

So case closed? Of course, we know that it's not really that easy, don't we? After all, we know from earlier in this book that deductive reasoning by its nature is definitional, and not necessarily meaningful. Recall the following:

> All fish are smelly
> Socrates is a fish
> Therefore, Socrates is smelly.

That the conclusion follows definitionally from the premises does not mean that anything of relevance is being said. How do we even know that the premises or their conclusion actually *apply* to anything? This, I think, is the strongest criticism to any non-empirical argument (and, therefore, it's hardly a unique criticism to my argument alone). Whether we're talking about theories of the big bang, the origins of life, black holes, dark matter, etc., without empirical evidence there can always remain the nagging question of whether or not such theories actually apply to anything that's real. Even if it's accepted that 1, ∅ is a fundamental distinction that, by definition, cannot be further reduced, it empirically cannot be proven that this distinction shows up upon the erasing of the Cosmic Eraser.

While acknowledging such inherent logical and empirical limitations, perhaps it would be apt for me to point out here how elegant and how simple my theory is, and how much sense it makes. Such a move on my part would unabashedly be attempting to pull at your human intuition. Should we just *assume* that our human intuition is trustworthy? What if yours happens to be different from mine? And, hey, I can't be trusted anyway—and you can trust me when I say that. Or perhaps it would be apt for me to point out here how my theory meets all my initial criteria regarding what constitutes a successful theory of existence. For instance, it 1) enhances the scientific viewpoint, 2) enhances the mystical viewpoint, and 3) offers a different and *other than* interpretation for what constitutes existence. I could also wax on about how my theory predicts quantum potentiality in vacuum states by interpreting it as but a shadow copy of the Theme. However, my opinion is nothing more than my opinion and you wouldn't really think that I'd present a set of criteria in direct conflict with my argument now would you?

In a way, my argument is kind of like saying, "well, since *such and such* is defined as *so and so*, it therefore follows that *how do you do*." This algorithm is a piece of logic that depends upon the definitions of words. We're traveling on similar grounds as already taken with the ontological argument as we've discussed before. Recall how some have argued that based upon how "Perfect Being" is defined, such a being therefore must actually exist (as, otherwise, how could it be perfect?). Well, it seems reasonable to ask if I'm really doing anything much different.

Actually, yes I am. For starters, I'm not presuming a loaded concept such as "Perfect Being," or anything even remotely equivalent to such a concept. Instead, I have logically reduced concepts about nature to reveal a basic distinction that has really been there all along. I'm not introducing anything new by saying, "the *possibility of a possibility* and *not even that* is the most fundamental distinction about nature that's logically possible." The claim is a direct consequence of the concepts already involved. It's simply a fact that based upon what a *possibility of a possibility* and *not even that* mean, these concepts must therefore represent a fundamental distinction that cannot be further reduced.

Now here's the important part: While the distinction of a *possibility of a possibility* and *not even that* is a logical distinction, notice that the concepts involved cannot help but be descriptions of nature. We know immediately that a quantum vacuum, a Chevy Silverado, and a Ding Dong, all fall under the category of *possibility of a possibility*. This is definitional. In comparison, while I grant that the attribute of existence is implied from the concept of a "Perfect Being" such that for a being to actually be perfect it would have to exist, it doesn't therefore follow that there is such a perfect being necessitating its own existence. Nature could run its course whether or not there actually was a being that was perfect. This is quite different from my argument as it's logically impossible for nature to not fall under one of two categories; 1) *the possibility of a possibility*, and 2) *not even that*. By definition, nature *has to* fall under one of these two categories, whereas nature is under no obligation whatsoever to produce a Being that is perfect.

Is The Script Falsifiable?

A possible disclaimer to my theory is that The Script is *unfalsifiable*, meaning that it's impossible to prove false and so is suspect by nature. In efforts of providing an example to the meaning behind "falsifiability," consider the following analysis by the physicist Victor Stenger:

> Early in this century, the philosopher of science Karl Popper grappled with the problem of distinguishing science from pseudoscience. He realized that science is not simply a matter of explaining already well-established empirical observations after the fact; pseudosciences, such as astrology, do that. He proceeded to compare four revolutionary developments that were in progress at that time, all labeled "scientific" by their promoters. There were: (1) Einstein's general theory of relativity; (2) Marx's theory of history; (3) Freud's psychoanalysis; and (4) Alfred Adler's "individual psychology."

> Popper tells how excited he became when, in 1919, Arthur Eddington confirmed Einstein's prediction that light from a star would be bent in passing by the sun. He compared this specific, quantitative result with the qualitative and untestable claims being made in the other three areas and concluded: "I felt that these other three theories, though posing as sciences, had in fact more in common with primitive myths than with science; that they resembled astrology rather than astronomy." (Popper, 1987)

What made the difference in Popper's mind? In a sense, these theories were too explanatory. Popper observed that, in the minds of the supporters of Marx, Adler, and Freud, the three theories explained everything within their respective fields. They had the effect of an "intellectual conversion or revelation, opening your eyes to a new truth hidden from those not yet initiated." The truth of these theories was self-evident to the converted. They were more religion than science. Far from providing no evidence, verification was found everywhere one looked. (Stenger, *Physics and Psychics*)

Similarly, the philosopher Bryan Magee has this to say:

> Popper was never in doubt that the secret of the enormous psychological appeal of these various theories lay in their ability to explain everything. To know in advance that whatever happens you will be able to understand it gives you not only a sense of intellectual mastery but, even more important, an emotional sense of secure orientation in the world. Acceptance of one of these theories had, he observed, "the effect of an intellectual conversion or revelation, opening your eyes to a new truth hidden from those not yet initiated. Once your eyes were thus opened you saw confirming instances everywhere: the world was full of *verifications* of the theory…" (Magee, *Karl Popper*)

I've selected these particular quotes for a very pointed reason; to show that a theory's strength can only be measured by how well it performs under intense scrutiny, lest it be found to be "astrology rather than astronomy." Therefore, as I've done throughout this BYTE, I think it's very important to be precise when presenting a possible criticism to my own argument. After all, it has to be the sort of criticism that people would actually find reasonable enough to accept (as a "straw man" would not be acceptable to anyone, and therefore refuting it does not prove anything). The question, accordingly, is whether or not The Script falls victim to Popper's analysis: Is The Script *definitionally unfalsifiable*? Does it merely contain "qualitative and untestable claims" therefore offering only some sort of religious perspective?

Well, certainly my Script-theory requires the acceptance of certain premises. However, so long as those premises are accepted, I believe my theory withstands the summary rejection of being unfalsifiable. To hold otherwise would be like saying "since the statement 'a square has four sides' is unfalsifiable, it's

therefore meaningless." That's not what Popper had in mind. By definition, a square simply *has* to have four sides. Empirically verifying that this is true for every single square that one may come across has no bearing on the fact that a square is defined as a finite structure possessing four equal sides. I suggest that the concepts of *possibility of a possibility* and *not even that*, when viewed as the most basic distinction possible, deductively leads to the indeterminate conflict of [1 and Ø] **AND/OR** [1 or Ø]. So long as that premise is held to be true, then there cannot be any other Standard applied to it. The Law of non-Contradiction (or any other Standard) would be an *extra* that would violate the premise that the *possibility of a possibility* and *not even that* are the most basic of distinctions possible. No other Standard can be introduced here because that would imply that the *possibility of a possibility* and *not even that* actually were not the most basic of distinctions. It's like that most famous deductive argument of all:

> All men are mortal
> Socrates is a man
> Therefore, Socrates is mortal.

So long as the first two premises are true, the conclusion has to follow. But that's only if we accept the premises. If we assume that Socrates was a Space Alien, or that some men can be immortal, then it obviously would not follow that Socrates is in fact mortal. Likewise, if we assume that the *possibility of a possibility* and *not even that* are in fact not the most basic distinction possible, that would render the conclusion of [1 and Ø] **AND/OR** [1 or Ø] inapplicable. I maintain that the distinction I'm describing cannot help but encompass all possible scenarios of reality, and *because of this* reality is forced to follow this logical path. Regardless, note that this part of my argument is analytical in the same way that the Socrates argument is analytical. So long as the premises are true, the conclusion must follow, by definition. This is a matter of logic, and direct empirical verification, admittedly impossible in this situation, does not and cannot change its outcome.

However, my idiosyncratic idea of A Variation on a Theme is not analytic. Therefore, the criticism of unfalsifiability *is* applicable. So then, is A Variation on a Theme falsifiable?

Actually, I think it is capable of being disproven. After all, A Variation on a Theme aligns itself squarely with a *messy-computational* view of reality, with one of its primary claims being that (unconscious) experience has to be built into the universe. The idea of A Variation on a Theme suggests that the *how* of experience is secondary to its overwhelming potentiality. The potentiality comes first; the specific route taken is a frozen accident. The fact that carbon-based organisms happen to be the only examples of experience currently known is regarded as secondary to the fact that the universe *has to* contain a potentiality for experience. Carbon-based organisms simply turned out to be the most convenient and workable material available for nature's blind Varying. There should not be anything magical or intrinsically special about carbon-based organisms. Carbon-based organisms just happened to work.

So then, if it should turn out that we never discover non-Carbon based organisms or if machine experience is proven impossible, then that would count as a *falsification* of A Variation on a Theme. That's because the fundamental claim of A Variation on a Theme is that there's nothing intrinsically special about experience. It *has to* happen. Indeed, if it were ever shown that machine experience is impossible, then that would show, to my mind, that A Variation on a Theme is a *plainly incorrect* way of looking at things (meaning that it's unworkable).

As to any supposed "religious meaning" that the idea of A Variation on a Theme might have, I rather think that it provides none (at least in any feel-good, fuzzy way). It's simply a description (obviously, a very *approximate* description) of how things *had to* (and perhaps *have to*) unfold. However, an order to things previously unordered is undeniably provided which is at least psychologically pleasing. But that's not particularly a knock for or against my theory, since we cannot assume that the order our brains crave isn't somehow tied to a deeper order out of which it was first made possible.

As to whether or not A Variation on a Theme should be viewed as *interpretational* and *poetic*, I can only respond that it offers a picture of how the world works. If you want to call it *interpretational* and *poetic*, I'm inclined to agree. Note, however, that natural selection can be called the very same thing, and the principle of natural selection remains an important concept regardless of some lingering skepticisms. Besides, I don't think calling my Variation on a Theme theory interpretational and poetic is necessarily be such a bad thing. Consider the philosopher Bryan Magee's view on the subject:

> Although professional philosophers nowadays are often highly skilled in matters of argument, it is in the nature of things that not many of them can be expected to have original insights. The outcome is hundreds of books which are well argued but have little or nothing to say

that has not been said before. And because the quality of the argumentation is the only distinguished thing about them, and also the thing their readers as well as their writers are best at, it becomes the object of interest, and hence the criterion by which they and their authors are judges. In consequence, many professional philosophers and their students slide unthinkingly into proceeding as if philosophy is *about* arguments, and they lose sight of the fact that it is really about insights. (Magee, *The Philosophy of Schopenhauer*)

By presenting my idiosyncratic idea of A Variation on a Theme, I'm in effect presenting a deep, personal insight into the nature of how the world works. If that's taken to be *odd* or *uncommon*, that's not so much a criticism of my theory as it is an indictment of modern-day philosophical thought.

Where's the Beef?

While the Script of [1 & Ø] &/OR [1 or Ø] does not exactly *shimmer* with a life of its own, I believe it represents a fundamental law or principle of reality—an algorithmic process *that cannot not be*. It is this process, this conflict, that produces a spark, and once we have a spark the cosmological sciences can be brought into non-question begging play (i.e., we're no longer faced with such nonstarters as *how did there get to be a "first place" in the first place?*).

The conflict presented by [1 & Ø] &/OR [1 or Ø] is neither "God" nor "Chance." It is a *necessarily random/randomly necessary* algorithmic process. How can something be necessarily random/randomly necessary? Consider the following examples:

One day Wheeler was unwittingly subjected to a variant of the game of twenty questions. Recall that, in the conventional game, the players agree on a word and the subject tries to guess the word by asking up to twenty questions. Only yes-no answers can be given. In the variant version, Wheeler began by asking the usual questions: Is it big? Is it living? etc. At first the answers came quickly, but as the game went on they became slower and more hesitant. Eventually he tried his luck: "Is it a cloud?" The answer came back: "Yes!" Then everyone burst out laughing. The players revealed that to trick Wheeler no word had been chosen in advance. Instead they agreed to answer his questions purely at random, subject only to consistency with previous answers. Nevertheless, an answer was obtained. This obviously contingent answer was not determined in advance, but neither was it arbitrary: its nature was decided in part by the questions Wheeler chose to ask, and in part by pure Chance.

And on a more intentionally silly note (and it's not as if the world doesn't contain *that* quality!):

> Only the fool would take trouble to verify that his sentence was composed of ten a's, three b's, four c's, four d's, forty-six e's, sixteen f's, four g's, thirteen h's, fifteen i's, two k's, nine l's, four m's, twenty-five n's, twenty-four o's, five p's, sixteen r's, forty-one s's, thirty-seven t's, ten u's, eight v's, eight w's, four x's, eleven y's, twenty-seven commas, twenty-three apostrophes, seven hyphens, and, last but not least, a single! (as appearing in Hofstadter's *Metamagical Themas*)

These analogies demonstrate how something can seem to *unfold spontaneously*, yet be completely *pre-determined*. In the former case, the very act of Wheeler's unwitting participation in such a rigged 20 Questions game demands that any given question he may ask (no matter how outlandish) will directly influence the impending conclusion. Likewise, in the latter case, so long as an author takes it upon himself to write a sentence that meticulously numbers its own characters, then in accordance with those arbitrary rules, at least a Variation of *this particular end-result* is imminent.

Such analogies speak not of God, nor of Chance; they speak of both. They speak of *paradox*. I think this exemplifies the sort of start-up procedure that must have occurred before we could even get to the *possibility* of a big bang. It was randomly, chaotically generated—following no pre-ordained plan—yet it had to happen precisely the way that it did due to the fundamental principle/s involved.

A Variation Compared

Recall our prior discussion on memes. Memes are to be viewed as mindless replicators for ideas. Just as animal genes could not come to existence until the evolution of plants, so too the memes could not come to existence until the evolution of animals had stumbled upon that noble beast called *Homo sapiens*. These

memes take shelter inside our brains and provide our very means of communication and idea making. The principle of natural selection determines which of these memes flourish, and which of these memes perish. Like a virus, they may infest many a mind through such modern contraptions as the media. They thrive and spread and vary and multiply. And Behold, *this very meme*—that which I'm communicating—is trying its best to infest yet another host.

Acknowledging that the meme theory is largely poetical, let's consider it in light of my idiosyncratic worldview of A Variation on a Theme. The theory of memes acknowledges the many enduring successful ideas such as God, the Prime Mover, "It from Bit," and the Eternal Return, all of which obviously precede my Variation on a Theme. My theory necessarily relies on these ideas as otherwise the concepts involved would have been incomprehensible. However, regardless of the origins, A Variation on a Theme is still a distinctly different meme from these predecessors. So then, how does it stack up against them?

Some may view my idea of A Variation on a Theme to be little more than a warmed-over Prime Mover or "it from bit." Well, for the rest of this Byte I'd like to take a look at these concepts and also some of the other theories possessing similarities to my worldview. Indeed, I have found quite a number of viewpoints that share likenesses, sometimes *striking likenesses*, to my worldview.

Biologist Stuart Kaufman and philosopher David Chalmers have somewhat recently presented *near*-identical arguments whereby they both independently asserted that some *outside condition* is necessary to fully explain *natural selection* and *consciousness* (as seen in *At Home in the Universe*, and *The Conscious Mind*). For Kaufman, this *outside condition* takes the form of a Self-Organizing principle. For Chalmers, this *outside condition* takes the form of some *brand-new* fundamental law that accounts for consciousness. Now I'm not in particular disagreement with what either of these two are saying, at least if looked at *abstractly enough*, however, when compared to what A Variation on a Theme is saying, there's—*at the very least*—one major difference.

Namely, I contend that the algorithmic process of natural selection *is the only* generator of Variation. According to A Variation on a Theme, natural selection works in a certain way because it's *forced* to work in a certain way. Again, my idea can be likened to Einstein's conception of a curved space-time whereby even a straight-line *cannot help but be curved* because space-time itself is curved. Well, I contend that natural selection cannot help but work as it does because it's part of a particular type of Variation on a necessarily existing Theme. There's no Design to any of this. There's No One up there "Pulling the Strings." There's no Mystical Force out there. Natural selection simply cannot help but follow *its own straightest line;* that "straightest line" being A Variation on a Theme. My argument eliminates the multiplicity of different fundamental theories (i.e., one for natural selection, one for consciousness, etc.), into the singular principle of A Variation on a Theme.

Let's also consider Plato's theory of Forms (also called "Ideas"). Since his theory of Forms has different versions, let's first make clear which version we'll be discussing. Sometimes Plato seems to speak of Forms as though they were little more than *sets,* such that, for example, all separate and individual chairs can be universally categorized under the Form of Chair. If this was all that his theory of Forms amounted to, then, in my opinion, it wouldn't be very significant. However, other times his theory of Forms, as seen in *The Timaeus* and *The Republic,* seems to be concerned with the concept of *necessity.* In these works, a Form is considered to be what's necessary (as in a necessary *pattern* or *prototype*), whereas the perceivable universe is somehow a shadowy copy of that Form. It's this version that has obvious similarities to A Variation on a Theme as evidenced by Plato's distinction between a *necessary Form* and a *copied world.* Fundamentally, I think that Plato's Forms as discussed in *The Timaeus* and *The Republic* and my Variation on a Theme can be interpreted as saying fundamentally the same thing. The obvious difference comes about when A Variation on a Theme is coupled with my analytical argument for the necessity of existence. Plato never spelled out how a necessary Form came to necessarily exist which is indeed a very significant difference from my position.

And, of course, when one mentions Plato, one must also mention...

Aristotle held that there was an unmoved source for all movement—God. In his *Physics,* Aristotle argues that movement must have a cause. Since an infinite regress is incomprehensible, there must then be a unique, unmoved source of movement—the Prime Mover. This Prime Mover was thought to be One, eternal, alive, immaterial, and to be Thought Thinking Itself. The 19th century German philosopher Friedrich Hegel varied this theory by suggesting that while there was such a thing as a Thought Thinking Itself, it was *not* metaphysically absolute. Rather, Thought Thinking Itself was something that was attained through the emergence and evolution of humanity. More recently, the 20th century philosopher Alfred North Whitehead proposed a *dipolar* God—a God that is both primordial and consequent. A God that is both the *unconscious* beginning, **and,** through the process of Creativity, the *conscious* End Result.

In a similar vein, 20th century physicist John Wheeler proposed an "it from bit"—referring to a self-excited universe that bootstraps itself into participatory existence. For Wheeler, the observed and unobserved undergo a sort of

mutually bewitching dance—with the unobserved helping to create us, and we helping to create the unobserved. In his own words, "every it—every particle, every field of force, even the space-time continuum itself—derives its function, its meaning, its very existence entirely—from the apparatus-elicited answers to yes or no questions, binary choices, *bits*." The "bit" is short for "binary digits," which are the type of numbers used by modern digital computers—regarded here to be as fundamental to reality as matter and energy. Perhaps the best evidence to support this is the *digital information* contained within DNA. This information does not degrade over time, no matter how many copies are made. DNA has obviously played (and continues to play) a very key role in natural selection. The success of certain types of technology—like compact disc's, laser disc's, and computers—also demonstrates the usefulness of viewing the world in terms of *bits*.

The "it from bit" theory is really suggesting that the universe is questioning itself (through us) and that with each and every self-response it grows closer and closer to the type of universe it must become in order that it can exist. This implies not only a privileged role for *us* but it also implies an anti-evolutionary, and ultimately anti-rational perspective. However, it may still be possible to water it down somewhat, by first assuming there to be an *it*, and then suggesting that consciousness only later arrives on the scene to play a substantial and dynamical role in the determination of what that *it* ultimately turns out to be.

The major difference between these views and mine, I believe, stems from how things originated. Instead of *thinking backwards* to get to the "Prime Mover" or having our thinking abilities actually create the *it* outright, my analytical argument explains the necessity behind such a thing in the first place—and why it must exist.

A Variation on a Theme also differs with physicist David Bohm's picture of an Implicate Order. In fact, I hope the reader agrees with me that while the picture Bohm presents may be pleasing (ultimately, a Russian Doll of implicate orders inside implicate orders), there is no *necessity* to be found anywhere. Why is it like that? How did it get there? One can talk all day about wholeness, order, and interconnection, but these concepts have no meaning in and of themselves. It needs to be shown *how* and *why* there's anything at all in the first place. This interpretation lacks necessity and is therefore itself lacking, at least when regarded as a theory of existence.

Similar to Bohm's view on everything being deeply interconnected, Fritjof Capra in his book *Tao of Physics*, writes:

In Mahayana Buddhism, a,..., cosmic network of interpenetrating things and events is illustrated in the Avaamsaka Sutra by the metaphor of Indra's net, a vast network of precious gems hanging over the palace of the god Indra. In the words of Sir Charles Eliot, "In the heaven of Indra, there is said to be a network of pearls, so arranged that if you look at one you see all the others reflected in it. In the same way each object in the world is not merely itself but involves every other object and in fact is everything else. "In ever particle of dust, there are present Buddhas without number."

Elsewhere Capra can only speak vaguely of "self-consistency" to go along with this picture of "interpenetrating things." For example, when he equates the eastern mystical vision with modern bootstrap theories (similar to the "it from bit" theory already discussed), he can only appeal to this self-consistency—"all particles are dynamically composed of one another in a self-consistent way..."—as if that alone can explain its existence. This is important. If it's stated, "there is no explanation!"—then, why isn't there an explanation? If there's no response to that, then perhaps nothing is really being said after all.

Parallels can also be drawn between my analytical argument and some of the ancient creation myths. Recall the Hindu origins myth from *The Rig-Veda* that we sampled earlier (here remixed compliments of a different translator):

Then was not non-existent nor existent: there was no realm of air, no sky beyond it. What covered in, and where? and what gave shelter? Was water there, unfathomed depth of water?

Death was not then, nor was there aught immortal: no sign was there, the day's and night's divider. That One Thing, breathless, breathed by its own nature: apart from it was nothing whatsoever....

He, the first origin of this creation, whether he formed it all or did not form it, whose eye controls this world in highest heaven, he verily knows it, or perhaps he knows not.

What an interesting thought: "He, the first origin of this creation, whether he formed it all or did not form it, whose eye controls this world in highest heaven, he verily knows it, or perhaps he knows not." Assuming that this means "a *paradox* cannot be fully known," it follows that this mystical experience (if indeed it was such) may have a striking similarity to the random-necessity that my analytical argument suggests.

In fact, my over-all view can be likened to a head-on collision—a *smashingtogether*—of mysticism and rationalism. The philosopher Arthur Schopenhauer accomplished, to my mind, much the same feat back in the 19th century. In his book, *The World as Will and Representation*, he melts together the Subject/Object dichotomy, showing that the one cannot exist without reference to the other, an insight to which I whole-heartedly agree (at least relative to our perspective!). Schopenhauer was openly influenced by Kant, Plato, and Eastern mysticism. From Kant he received the idea of the world as *representation* (meaning that there is no such thing, outside of a confused manner of speaking, as a world *without* perception). From Kant he also received the idea of a thing-in-itself as an underlying *something or other* from which the Subject arises. Schopenhauer identified this *something or other* with a *blindly impassioned* Will (as in a *will-to-live*). From Plato he received the idea of Forms such that he regarded this Will as an Object, a pattern, a template from which all representation is but a shadowy copy. This idea of a "shadowy copy" has much similarity (which Schopenhauer readily admits to) with the eastern mystical idea of *maya*. Like Plato's theory of Forms, the "world as maya" meant that the perceived world was but a shadowy copy of a deeper underlying Reality (whether called "Brahman," "Atman," "Will," or whatever else). The similarities should be obvious at this point between Schopenhauer's theory of Will (along with some of the influences from which he draws) to my Variation on a Theme (although I have no patience for his pronounced pessimism). The difference, however, is basic and quite decisive. I will *not accept* any interpretation of the world just for the sake of owning an interpretation of the world. If you say there's only matter, then how came there to be matter? If you say there's only mind, then how came there to be mind? If you say there's only will, then how came there to be will? Fundamentally, I want to know *how* and *why* nature became possible in the first place.

Author John Horgan wrote in his *The End of Science*, "the physicist John Wheeler,…, intuited…[that]…[a]t the very heart of reality lies not an answer, but a question: why is there something rather than nothing?" With all due respect, that's not the correct question. The question is "why *should* there be something rather than nothing, and vice-versa?" The difference is not merely semantics and word-play. It better gets across the fundamental ambiguity, the indeterminacy, the fragile necessity of all things. For how could such things be decided if not by default—by algorithmic paradox?

BYTE FIVE:

TIME

http://www.philscanlan.net/

Got Time?

Consider for a second how frequently we look down upon our watches, or how we steal a quick glance at a clock. Now let's say that this was "bad" for some reason, and that the Government ("the Man") in its wisdom somehow gave us an electrical shock whenever we were to glance at a watch or clock. Invariably, we would either be forced to familiarize ourselves with shock-therapy (and just deal with it), or we would be forced to cut back on a deeply ingrained habit (which I'd wager that most of us would not appreciate at all). "Time" is what keeps our schedules in order. It's what keeps our appointments. It's even what tells us when our favorite shows are on television. But *what is time*?

Clearly, upon *any* type of examination we have to conclude that *time is relative*. Anyway, that's what Einstein showed us earlier last century, or many centuries ago depending on when you finally get around to reading this book. He presented a rather simple thought experiment, although it took the genius of an Einstein to figure out that this was the *accurate* way of looking at things.

Basically, Einstein invited us to consider *any given event* involving movement—like a car passing by. Let's say that there's a sensor at a certain point in the road so that when the car passes over it, a bright light flashes. Now let's further say that there are three different observers: Looker1 next to the sensor holding a stopwatch, Looker2 in the car holding a stopwatch, and Looker3 in an overhead airplane holding a stopwatch. Due to the absolute nature of the speed of light, Einstein said that the *instant* the light flashed was going to be recorded at *three distinct times* relative to each one of the three Lookers. That's because each of the Lookers was forced to measure the speed it took the light signal to get to them relative to their respective positions. In essence, it wasn't *the speed of light* that varied (that was the constant), rather it was *the measurement of time* that varied for each one of the Lookers (the idea of an Absolute Time becoming meaningless). For Einstein, and for us all, time is a personal concept—a concept *dependent upon* and *relative to* each Looker that measures it.

Perhaps this thought experiment has lost much of its impact for us compared to what it must have been like when first introduced. That's because we become so familiarized, over time (ahem), to what was once a novel idea—that we sometimes forget how impressive an insight it originally was. There's a sort

of built-in attitude that develops—"well, *of course*, it works that way. How else would it work?"

The primary assumption that Einstein's thought experiment attacked dealt with the very notion of a Universal Time. You see, there's *no such thing* as a Universal Clock that can record an Absolute, Universal Time. That's because we cannot get *outside of time* to measure it. Instead, Einstein showed how time must be viewed as *relative* to each and every Looker and their respective motions *toward* and *away from* any given event.

This is not particularly intuitive. For one thing, it suggests that even if we were to chase after a beam of light at 2/3 the speed of light, and then measure the speed of that beam of light, we would not measure it at 1/3 the speed of light. The speed of light would still be constant; it's unchanging.

The speed of light is the foundation upon which Einstein constructed his theory of time. Einstein also demonstrated an interesting relationship between mass and time via the speed of light whereby the closer something approaches the speed of light, the more its mass increases and the more its clocks will slow down (at least relative to our clocks). This phenomenon leads us to the Twin Paradox. This paradox is a famous thought experiment suggesting that if one of a set of identical twins blasts off at near the speed of light to some distant star and then returns home, he will find himself to be years younger than his other half who remained home. This "years younger" is to be reflected in all meaningful definitions of the concept "time": From wrinkles and gray hairs, to calendars and subjective impressions. Indeed, if the star is distant enough the twin might return to Earth at a time when his twin no longer lives. In other words, *time travel really is possible.*

This defies common sense because, in all ordinary cases, identical twins are the exact same age from cradle to grave. However, physicists today regard the Twin Paradox as accepted fact—that's due to experiments that have since been done with extremely accurate clocks. In this regard, in 1972, the physicist Joseph Hafele established that passengers on commercial jetliners returned home a minuscule but measurable split second younger than any non-jetliner passenger. (Poundstone, 1988).

Notice that this time travel applies only to *going forward*; the difficulties of *going backward* are well-known and fraught with contradiction (e.g., how can you kill yourself from ten years past yet have lived in the future to travel back in time to kill yourself in the first place?). The notion of time travel with its many contradictions has a sort of eye-rolling quality to it. At least it does for me, as it has always seemed rather academic. But for the sake of argument, let's assume that we discover a "higher dimension" or a "worm-hole" (or *whatever*) that allows us to short-cut our way to another layer in the block of space-time. Are we then committed to a universe of contradictions?

Not necessarily, so long as we assume that any act of time-travel is an act of viewing another possible world. In one scenario, I could time travel to a possible world in which my mother's mother was killed by a freak time travel accident whereby my time-machine (in the form of a car or telephone booth, depending on your preference for movie references) accidentally landed on her. If I were to grow old in that world, I would find that neither my mother nor I would ever exist in it. My mother exists in that *other* world that I came from, not this current one. Again, I find all this not very compelling. But people seem to get a kick out of time travel, so there you go.

In efforts of better relating the *radicalness* of Einstein's idea, I invite you to consider the following *updated* version of Einstein's thought experiment. Let's start by imagining a Clock's Face on top of a full Moon. This Clock's Face is equipped with an hour hand, a minute hand, and even a second hand. As to why the Moon has a Clock's Face on it, let's just say that some people are going to have a lot of *time* on their hands in the future and will be spending it through the pursuit of pointless projects. So anyway, let's also suppose that it takes the approximate two seconds or so for the light from the Moon to strike our eyes. Intuitively, then, we can see that we'll always be looking at the Moon as it was a couple seconds *in the past*. Notice also that even if we use a *powerful telescope and zoom in real tight*, the light we'll be seeing the Moon with would still be a couple of seconds old.

Now, let's go one step further. Let's say that in the future a *super telescope* is developed that's capable of peering, with minute detail, at *another inhabited world*. Most of us already know that the light we see with from a star at night may actually be billions of years old, i.e. whenever we look up at the sky at night, *we're viewing the past* (I'm sure you can now see where I'm going with this).

Alright, so let's further say that when we view this inhabited world with our *super telescope* we see a bunch of beings stumbling around that seem a lot like us (or, if you prefer, they can appear to be *much, much* different from us). The upshot here is that it's clear we'd be viewing a planet-full of beings that have long since been dead. Now you may want to balk at this and suggest that we'd be watching some sort of a *light-show*, or a *simulation*—a simulation that wouldn't really be occurring "now." But that really misses the point. Einstein was suggesting that *from our point of view*, that "simulation" is as good as real. There's not a true distinction.

And, of course, just to stir things up a bit we can also flip this thought experiment around. We can say that the *far-off inhabited world* developed their own type of *super telescope* and that they're *peering at earth*. The only catch, of course, is that the earth they'd be viewing won't have us on it! Or would it?

Now who's right and who's wrong? Who's *really existing* and who's *not really existing*?

What this sort of thought experiment seems to imply is a space-time that exists as a block-whole. "Future" and "past" events exist simultaneously, and any event is available for viewing provided you're at the right perspective. So then, what we perceive to be the "passage of time" becomes illusory. Many scientists, I think incorrectly, believe that Einstein's theory of relativity implies the metaphysical illusoriness of our perceptions of time.

It's easy enough to play with words and whimsically label the passage of time as "illusory." But a deeper inquiry suggests that the entire artifice of a "relativistic time" is dependent on observers. Well, observers were not around at the big bang. Nor were they around on earth prior to the introduction of life. So then, if the passage of time is dependent upon observers, and since there's good evidence suggesting that the universe did not always contain observers, how can the early universe, along with our eventual evolution, be accounted for?

That's the intrinsic problem of an "appearance-driven" metaphysics—it's incapable of taking into account all the known evidence. Any observer existing in the universe must ultimately be created from the stuff of the universe such that at some point "in time" the stuff of the universe was not in the form of observers. That implies that we live in an object-driven universe (where "stuff" rules), not an observer-driven universe (where "participation" rules). An object-driven universe alone, however, doesn't seem to explain the relativistic qualities that arise once observers enter the scene.

As previously discussed, physicist John Wheeler is famous for proposing a participatory observer-driven universe (the "it from bit") that permits "backwards" causation such that modern people can "create" the initial happening of the big bang as they study it. In his own words,

> It from bit symbolizes the idea that every item of the physical world has at bottom—at a very deep bottom, in most instances—an imma-
> terial source and explanation; that what we call reality arises in the
> last analysis from the posing of yes-no questions and the registering
> of equipment-evoked responses; in short, that all things physical are

information-theoretic in origin and this is a participatory universe. (Wheeler, 1996)

The most satisfying aspect of his theory is how it explains one of the more paradoxical characteristics of quantum mechanics—"delayed choice." This phenomenon was first recognized by Neils Bohr, one of the founders of quantum theory. The phenomenon of delayed choice suggests—and experiments repeatedly verify—that even though a photon might have began its journey some six billion years ago, no polarization or direction of vibration can be ascribed to it until an observer "nudges" it one way or the other. As Wheeler put it,

> Not until the analyzer has been set to this, that, or the other specific chosen orientation; not until the elementary quantum phenomenon that began so long ago—and stretches out, unknown and unknowable, like a great smoky dragon through the vast intervening reach of space and time—has been brought to a close by an irreversible act of amplification; not until a record has been produced of either "yes, this direction of polarization" or "no, the contrary direction of polarization"; not until then do we have the right to attribute any polarization to the photon that began its course so long ago.

To an extent, the life of a photon can be viewed a fuzzy one, a super-posited state of nondefinition, *until* an observer comes along and sharpens it into focus. This leads to the speculation that existence is a matter of degree whereby an existing thing like a photon grows more focused and "real" when a greater level of consciousness becomes involved. Of course, the original interpretation that got us to such heights of dizzying contemplation is probably wrong.

The delayed choice phenomenon is better interpreted as a sort of "optical illusion" produced by a patched-together artifact, an imperfect brain that simply cannot get a firm grip on the events involved. Well, at least I find that far more likely than the idea that we have god-like powers of creation! We didn't create ourselves and our minds do not possess any mystical, god-like powers. We are a function of the universe and we should not be used as the explanation for the existence of the universe. And this is precisely what Wheeler ends up doing. He suggests that other possible universes exist only in a "weak" sense of logical possibility, any "strong" sense necessitating a life and consciousness in that universe at some point, however briefly. The implication is that consciousness ends up "creating" the big bang (by mystically converting the big bang

from a fuzzy possibility to a sharpened reality) as it looks back and studies the beginnings of the universe (i.e., physicists create the universe!). Truly, that's what he's ultimately saying. And it's just not very satisfying.

Conceptually, I believe the big picture of time can once again be likened to that young woman/old woman optical illusion example from BYTE ONE. We have a paradoxical universe that is as much observer-driven as it is object-driven, and we're stuck trying to interpret it as *either* observer-driven *or* object-driven. The problem lies entirely with our inadequate evolutionarily patched-together brains. We are incapable of visualizing a paradoxical situation whereby the universe can be both object-driven *and* observer-driven at one and the same time. We want to make false distinctions in efforts of making the situation easier to understand. But just like a photon can be both a wave and a particle, I believe that "time" is as much an object-driven phenomenon as it is an observer-driven phenomenon. I believe that "stuff rules" just as much as "observers rule." You can't get observers without stuff, and there can't be stuff without observers. So how can we wrap our faulty brains around this one?

Quite frankly, the only way that this conflict can be resolved is by admitting that Einstein's Observer-dependent notion of time is not the only way of describing time. The theory of relativity is *the* scientific way of viewing time, but it's not a supportable metaphysical way because it depends on observers. Since "time" elapsed in the universe prior to the arrival of observers, we are left with the realization that the theory of relativity provides a less-than-complete rendition of time, and should therefore not be treated metaphysically (which is a trap that I think many science-pundits fall into). Note that this is not a criticism of Einstein, as he presented a *scientific* theory, not a *metaphysical* theory. It is a criticism of later pundits who turned the theory of relativity into metaphysics.

A more comprehensive *metaphysical* way of viewing time is as an algorithmic variation on a theme. Our universe varies the theme of the self-writing Script, chugging away through its iterations of theme-varying: ultimately resulting in great complexity. An algorithm is a process, and a process moves. And we, as conscious experiencers inside the algorithm, perceive the movement and are part of the algorithmic movement and call it "time."

BYTE SIX:
NATURAL SELECTION

http://www.philscanlan.net/

2004 by Phil V. Scanlan

The Natural Algorithm

The theory of natural selection ranks as perhaps the greatest intellectual revolution in human history. Charles Darwin drastically changed our world-view by giving the idea of evolution a body of evidence along with a coherency that it never had previously.

By the 19th century, geologists were beginning to understand the full significance of *strata*—the layers of sediment deposits. This layering seemed to imply a time sequence, with the younger strata overlying older strata. By the 1830s, influential geologist (and unequalled propagandist) Charles Lyell won major support for the concept of *uniformitarianism*—the working hypothesis that the present conditions and processes of the earth are the keys to what happened in the past. The study of strata soon became deeply influenced by this new way of thinking.

However, anomalous fossil discoveries started to add up during the 18th and 19th centuries. At first, naturalists assumed they were finding remains of unknown but still living species, keeping in line with their strict uniformitarian interpretation. But dinosaur bones sure didn't look like any presently living species. As early as 1800, French naturalist Georges Cuvier (considered by many the father of paleontology) connected deeper stratas with less familiar-looking fossils. This alone provided a working idea of evolution for many in that era. But the idea was still being developed, and there were varying interpretations. Lamarck's failed attempt at explaining evolution is the most famous, and history has been unkind (and perhaps unfair) to him.

As early as 1801, French naturalist Jean-Baptiste Lamarck proposed a mechanism for adaptive change based on the inheritance of acquired characteristics. Infamously, he believed that the necks of Giraffes became long as a result of continual stretching to reach high leaves. He would have been on much firmer ground had his example of acquired characteristics involved only *behavior*, not form, as behavioral characteristics can be passed on through *learning*, but form cannot. His example of *change in form* is what has been attacked and ridiculed.

In 1831, Charles Darwin sailed to the Galapagos Islands in the HMS Beagle. He was fascinated by the slight variations between tortoises from different islands and how a whole array of unique finches exhibited slight differences from island to island. He noticed how the theme had varied. It wasn't until

1858 that Darwin published his *On the Origin of Species* (some 50 years after Lamarck's earlier attempt). This provided ample time for the maturation of his idea, as well as the accumulation of extensive supporting evidence. Since its publication, Darwin's book has met with controversy. To this day, a recurring suggestion has been made, in differing forms, that an alternative to natural selection, based on an "Intelligent Design" hypothesis, should be presented on equal grounds for the young and impressionable student.

Darwin's theory of evolution can be outlined as follows:

- Organisms tend to *change* over time, and the ones living today are different from those that lived in the past. And many more still that lived in the past have simply become extinct.

- Change is typically gradual and slow to the point of being nonexistent so long as an appropriate niche is found (that's why a bacterium is a bacterium and a shark is a shark). When environmental conditions stress the organism's niche such that survival is threatened, then episodes of (relatively) rapid change punctuate the long periods of stasis for those lucky organisms possessing *make-do* characteristics allowing them to survive and eventually adapt to the new situation. This latter theory is known as *punctuated equilibrium*, and adds a nice wrinkle to Darwin's predominantly gradualistic process (as Darwin was deeply influenced by Lyell).

- Organisms derive from common ancestors.

- The mechanism of evolutionary change was *natural selection*.

Natural selection is a process that occurs over successive generations. The following summarizes Darwin's line of reasoning for how it works.

- Unbounded population growth resembles a simple geometric series (2-4-8-16-32-64...), quickly reaching infinity.

- Since not all species can enjoy an unbounded growth in this manner, it logically follows there is a metaphorical "struggle" to survive and reproduce, in which only a few are "saved" in the program of life.

- Parents possessing traits better enabling them to survive and reproduce will produce more offspring than those not possessing such traits.

- These offspring differ slightly from their parents and from one another.

- To the extent that offspring resemble their parents, the population in the next generation will consist of a higher proportion of individuals that possess whatever adaptation enabled their parents to survive and reproduce.

Adding strength to the above analysis, *genetics* became incorporated into the mechanism of natural selection during the early and middle 20th Century, providing a greatly needed *mechanism* for Darwin's abstract process of natural selection.

The theory of heredity is attributed to Gregor Mendel (1823-1884), based on his work with pea plants. Mendel's work has since become the foundation for modern genetics. His work was so ahead of its time that it took over thirty years for the rest of the scientific community to catch on. The major problem hindering immediate acceptance dealt *not* with Mendel's meme, which was brilliant, but rather the person presenting the meme. Mendel was hardly a world-renowned scientist of his day. In fact, he was an Augustinian monk who taught natural science to high school students. His love of nature led him to carry out many experiments from which he saw that traits were inherited in certain numerical ratios. From such experiments, Mendel derived certain basic laws of heredity that retain to this day: hereditary factors (now called "genes") do not combine, but are passed along intact; each member of the parental generation transmits only half of its hereditary genes to each offspring (with certain genes "dominant" over others); and different offspring of the same parents receive different sets of hereditary genes.

Darwin did not, and perhaps could not, account for the modern theory of genetic micro-mutations in his theory of evolution, but it is upon Darwin's framework of natural selection that the modern synthesis rests. Before moving away from natural selection, there are two very important points to specifically highlight. First, *not all living things gradually change over time*. Most living things—like bacteria—stay the same, or very nearly the same, on a seemingly permanent basis. Evidently, once a living thing enters a *successful niche*, there is no need for further change. What determines a successful niche? Evidently, *survival*. Notice that this is in sharp contrast to the idea that natural selection undergoes a *continual* rate of change in any and all species. That is simply not true. A species does not evolve into another species because it *wants to* or because some force moves it to. A species evolves into another if and only if the circumstances in

which the species finds itself demands such an evolvement for its continued survival. Computationally speaking, if a random mutation favoring survival in a stressed environment does not affect at least one organism in the species that can replicate itself and multiply, then that species will no longer exist. That's the Program of Life.

Second, the process of natural selection is best viewed as a giant, purposeless algorithm. To illustrate, a mechanical watch requires all of its components to be in place in order to function, and therefore requires a "creator." Contrast this to the modern human eye which is much more complex than a watch. An oft-repeated argument has been that something as complex as the human eye demands a creator. Not necessarily so. Rather, we're dealing here with; variation, recursiveness, and cumulation. Even if I saw the world in a most hazy manner, with eyes that were little more than "sensitive warts," that would still be greatly beneficial over *not seeing at all*. Hence, an eye can form a cumulative step at a time, with each new step possessing an advantage over its predecessor.

The real power of natural selection lies in the fact that it recursively builds upon already successful "models" by mechanically varying the theme. When we pull back and look at the results over Time, we see a natural program; a blind algorithm.

Some four centuries ago Francis Bacon urged the philosophers of his day to abandon the attempt of showing how the universe arose from thought, and rather to consider how thought arose from the universe. The blind algorithm is a way by which Bacon's suggestion can be made reality.

Inside the program of natural selection, perhaps the most significant characteristic of any living thing is its ability to replicate, since if it didn't have that ability then it wouldn't be around for long. It would be "deleted" from the program. Consider the mindless replications of molecular organisms. These molecular organisms perform tasks, including replication, as *if they were agents of their actions*. Yet, it seems far-fetched to claim that these things really comprehend why it is they perform the actions that they do. In much the same way, we are also agents of action—we're just more complex, and more *comprehending*. However, I dare say we are not *that* different. After all, do we not owe our very existence to an instinctual necessity of replication? And do we not also have many processes in our machine-like bodies that are blind and instinctual? Or are we really in control of our digestive systems, our antibodies, and the billions of neurons inside our brains? Are we really in control of each and every cell in our human body—cells that seem to mindlessly carry on their little tasks, *as if they were agents of action*? Are we really in control of our *urge to replicate*, to reproduce? True, there's an obvious *difference* between us and them, yet it is a difference bounded by a profound *similarity*.

If we choose to grant this similarity, the commonality between us and them would seemingly have to be that of natural selection. Natural selection is probably best viewed as an interplay between us fundamentally blind-mutating-replicators, and the environment. This process is *not* without friction. Much like a feather does not fall as swiftly as a rock when dropped *here on earth*, the randomness of natural selection encounters its own friction. If the random mutations are not beneficial within the organism's environment then those mutations will not survive to replicate. This interplay must be granted. It's a predominantly gradual and cumulative process, and a powerful process at that. And it works by default.

The default process of random replication set against the friction of an environment is not, in and of itself, an explanatory device for the human qualities of awareness and thought. A *Just So* theory is unhelpful and offers us little more than warmed-over mythology: as in *things are **Just So** because natural selection and the environment caused them to be **Just So**.*

An interesting example of a *Just So* program is represented by the Aquatic Ape Theory (AAT) expounded by Elaine Morgan. Her view is that *Homo sapiens* descended from an intermediate species that was aquatic. The reason this is brought up is because it's easy to explain why we resemble the African apes. Scientists can just point out that gorillas, chimpanzees and humans share a common ancestor. But it is much more difficult to explain why we differ from the gorilla and the chimpanzee much more markedly than they differ from one another. Something must have happened to cause us to proceed along an entirely different evolutionary path.

Morgan's idea is that flooding cut off a portion of our early ancestors from their cousins, forcing them to live by the shores—learning to dive for shellfish and other eats. But before fully evolving into the equivalent of dolphins, whales, or seals, circumstances changed once again. And so we are now a species left with "scars"—otherwise inexplicable remnants of a very distant past. A sampling of these scars reads as follows: our upright, bipedal posture; our layer of fat and propensity for obesity; and our relative hairlessness, perspiration, tears, and inability to respond to salt depravation in standard mammalian ways. These are all characteristics common among aquatic animals, but not so for land dwellers. The orthodox Savannah Theory, as taught in schools, doesn't satisfyingly account for any of these characteristics.

In short, it's not at all clear that the orthodox view describes a process *that actually happened.* Yet, over the years the position has solidified into a full-blown scientific consensus so that a viable alternative theory is ignored.

Okay, so we've considered an example of a specific "*Just So* program" running inside the larger program of natural selection. The Aquatic Ape Theory gives us at least a possible account for some of the differences us humans have compared to our closest evolutionary relatives. But there's still our most curious and compelling characteristic of all—consciousness—that has yet to be discussed. Now you're probably beginning to see why I guided you through the hopefully familiar terrain of natural selection: to introduce the related concept of *functionalism* and what it tells us about our *consciousness.*

BYTE SEVEN:

Consciousness

http://www.philscanlan.net/

Are You Experienced?

There's a Zen story of Nan-in, a 19th century Japanese Master, who was visited by a university professor inquiring about Zen. While Nan-in prepared tea for his visitor, the professor expounded at length on his personal philosophies and insights. Nan-in filled the professor's cup and kept right on pouring. With tea spilling all over, the professor exclaimed "It is full, no more will go in."

"Like this cup," Nan-in said, "you are already full of your own opinions and speculations. How can I show you Zen unless you first empty your cup?"

This parable applies to myself as much as to the reader. While researching this topic, reading from many perspectives at once (philosophy, psychology, physics, neurology, *The Far Side*) all the while trying to formulate some brilliantly insightful way of presentation, I managed to work myself into a psychological stale-mate: paralysis by analysis (my cup was overflowing). The subject-matter was so expansive and my ambitions so grand, I was unable to begin. And then I laughed at my predicament. How silly. That was all psychology—my own sense of self *trapping* myself into immobility! This is the starting point of my enquiry; my own self-conscious fallibility. And it's a surprisingly rich starting point.

Curiously, it seems to provide an explanation for the "self-destruct mechanism" illustrated by Howard Bloom in his *Global Brain*—easily the most intriguing example given for the Alpha position that the *group* supposedly has over the *individual* in the process of natural selection:

> A primal imperative to save one's self underlay the concept of "the fight or flight" syndrome hinted at by William McDougall in 1908 and popularized by Walter Cannon in 1915. However, as research psychologist Robert E. Thayer says, "certain aspects of the fight or flight response were never supported by scientific evidence." What's more, creatures confronted with an overwhelming threat are frequently paralyzed by anxiety, resignation, and fear, In other words, instead of fighting or fleeing for their lives, real-world inhabitants often leave themselves open to the jaws of death and let themselves be hauled away as prey. David Livingstone, of "Dr. Livingstone, I presume" fame, describes the actual sensation:

"I saw the lion just in the act of springing upon me…. He caught my shoulder as he sprang, and we both came to the ground below together. Growling horribly close to my ear, he shook me as a terrier does a rat. The shock produced a stupor similar to that which seems to be felt by a mouse after the first shake of the cat. It caused a sort of dreaminess in which there was no sense of pain, nor feeling of terror, though [I was] quite conscious of all that was happening. It was like what patients partially under the influence of chloroform describe, who see the operation but feel not the knife.

The implication is that since the individual is not busy saving himself, he must be busy sacrificing himself (for the greater good of the group). Now, my life was never at stake and my body never "shut itself off" in a *physiological* paralysis. It was only my mind that seemed to "shut off" in a mere *psychological* paralysis. Despite the obvious differences, I think the phenomena are related. A sense of being over-whelmed, heightened by fear caused by the nature of the given predicament, results in a state of *hysterical paralysis*. [I'm reminded of a *Cheers* TV show where Cliff, that hapless eternal bachelor, finds himself in a new relationship with a woman causing him to experience "hysterical blindness," thus destroying any possible chance he had in the relationship!] The "greater good" was nowhere to be found in the unwanted psychological paralysis that befell me. And, quite frankly, neither do I think it's anywhere to be found in examples of physiological paralysis. Animals are not perfect machines and it's a bit of a cheat to imagine that they should have perfect survival reflexes.

Still, what's the point of any of this? Is there truly some mysterious selective advantage of spinning thoughts in your own head so grandly as to become immobile? My hysterical experience of psychological paralysis presents a dividing line between function and experience; the processes that operate behind the scene, and the 1st person experience of those processes.

I hope the reader sees the humor in this situation as much as I, along with the deep human quality that it illustrates. We are fallible. Our vaunted intelligences oft-times prove to be our own downfall. We continually rationalize our participation in self-destructive behavior like cheating, adultery, lies, back-stabbing—all in efforts of achieving some transient, psychological need.

Our lives are based on those psychological needs, those imperfections. That's what it is to be conscious; to have a human mind.

What is mind? No matter.

What is matter? Never mind.

If we weed out the philosophical significance from this fun pun, we pretty much get René Descartes infamous dualistic philosophy, where mind and body are interpreted as two distinct *substances*. The substance of mind was thought to be special; not located in space, not an extended thing like matter. The Achilles Heel of this view is summed up nicely by varying a phrase made famous by a Wendy's commercial, "Where's the link?" If mind and body really are two distinct substances, then how do they interact? Long ago, Descartes offered the Pineal Gland, which was as good a guess as any I suppose. But there *has* to be some link. If there really are two entirely distinct substances, body and mind, then why is there such a close connection between the two? Where's the connection?

We will see a modern-day revisiting of this with famed physicist Roger Penrose's attribution of consciousness to quantum microtubules. The problem is that quantum microtubules are all over the place, begging the question "so then, why is the brain so special?"

Philosopher Gilbert Ryle became famous in the 1930s by coining the phrase "ghost in the machine," a particularly catchy and telling take on dualism. He is also well known for declaring that dualism makes a *category mistake*. According to Ryle, a category mistake is equivalent to someone mistakenly allocating the "University" to the same category as its collection of colleges, laboratories and offices.

I start here with Descartes and dualism's difficulties because that theory is what's found most appealing to our patched-together and imperfect brains. Obviously, we need to be very, very careful (as E. Fudd might say) with what we take to be obvious and intuitive. We weren't designed to understand any of this!

Sparks Alive!

As philosopher Richard Swinburne would ask: Why is there gravity? Why does man have two eyes instead of three? Why are there laws of nature? Why are these laws constant? Why do some chemical combinations produce life while most others do not? How does a brain evolved to a certain complexity give rise to consciousness? Why do certain brain events give rise to the specific mental states that they do? Why does brain event x cause a blue image, and brain event y a red image? Why does eating chocolate bring about a brain state resulting in the taste we call chocolatey, *every time*, and not some other random brain state resulting in various different tastes at different occasions?

Perhaps early humans originally thought that fire was *non*reproducible. Perhaps they thought that fire was something that *just happened* during lightning storms and other natural occurrences. However this may be, through trial and error fire was eventually reproduced. The *appropriate spark* is all that's required to reproduce fire. Can the same be said for mind? Is the reproduction of mind contingent upon the appropriate spark being found? If so, what could possibly account for that spark?

Fill-in-the-spark:

> An algorithm will evoke awareness when the special condition of _____ occurs.

The possible buzz-words to put here are *not* in short supply. "Higher-level organization," "universality," "self-reference" and "algorithmic simplicity/complexity" are all top contenders. (Penrose, 1994) Of these, self-reference is perhaps the closest in form to what I'm suggesting. Keep in mind, however, that self-reference in and of itself is inherently nonspecial. A camcorder can be positioned in front of a mirror—in fact, a *mirror* can be positioned in front of a mirror—and I would hesitate to conclude that anything remotely thoughtful is occurring. So then, what makes *our* type of self-reference suddenly so different?

Consciousness is as mysterious a subject as existence, and quite possibly closely related.

Consciousness is said to be identical to brain stuff; messy computation, nothing more. But the creatively inclined—writers, thinkers, mathematicians—know, they *know*, that they get deep insights pre-formed. Discovered. Not created. How is that possible? How can consciousness be messy-computation and yet otherwise smart people believe that insights are discovered, not created? How can there be a Truth beyond firing neurons?

Such questions don't quite jibe. The ideas of messy-computationalism and Platonism are *not* compatible. Yet an unbiased survey seems to include *both*, not either/or. Infuriating!

We're scratching something very deep with consciousness. Any sacredness that life might have is located right here. That's why the mysterians have such a hard time with the study of the brain. Because they believe that there's something special, something mysterious about life, about being alive, about being conscious. There's something wonderful about it. Sacred. Spiritual. I agree. For most people it all comes down to the simplistic equation of consciousness = the soul. If you take away the soul, there's nothing more to believe in. I understand this.

Functionalism

Functionalism, in a nutshell, holds that consciousness is to be identified not with a particular physical structure (like squishy gray brains or the particular neurons that the brains are made of), but rather with the functional organization of a system. The functionalist regards the human brain as an evolutionary artifact that just happens to possess a certain functional layout required for consciousness. The presumption is that the same functional layout should be possible by a computer program (for example), which would then make the computer conscious.

Significantly, functionalism implies that human-like mental states are not restricted to human-like biological systems, such as the brain. The *complexity* of the functional relationship is key. In this respect, our carbon-based form is viewed as an accident of history. Carbon-material happened to be the most pliable and responsive material for the Program of Life to blindly manipulate. Silicon *might* have worked had it been available in the early iterations of the Program of Life, except that it's too complex of a material to appear naturally. So, given the limited available materials, carbon happened to be the one that worked.

The principle model of computation that the modern day functionalist uses is that of the Turing machine. It all began in the 1930s (before the advent of the digital computer) when several mathematicians began experimenting with what it means to be able to compute a function. Alonzo Church and Alan Turing independently arrived at equivalent conclusions (isn't it funny how ideas have a way of "bubbling" up at the same time from different sources?). We might phrase their definition today as:

A function is computable if it can be computed by a Turing machine.

A Turing machine is an abstract representation of a computing device, but, logically speaking, it has all the power of any digital computer. It may be described as follows: A Turing machine processes an infinite tape, divided into squares, each of which is inscribed with a ∅ or a 1. At any time, the Turing machine has a read/write head positioned at some square on the tape. Computation begins with the machine scanning a square. It erases what it finds there, prints a ∅ or 1, moves to a bordering square, and thus goes into a new state, its actual behavior depending upon a table of instructions that it follows.

A Turing machine can be regarded as an idealized, abstracted computer program (software), more so than a computer itself (hardware). Computer scientists and logicians have shown that Turing machines—given enough time and tape—can compute any function that conventional digital computers can *possibly* compute. Hence, most functionalists assume that if consciousness is computable, then it can be computed by a Turing machine. And that's why there's such a widespread belief among functionalists that someday computers will be able to attain consciousness.

An obvious question arises here; how would we ever know that a computer became conscious even if it did?

The best test as of now for determining machine-awareness is the Turing Test (yes, from the same Alan Turing). Basically, the Turing Test suggests that *human-like responses to questions implies human-like awareness*. This test is performed much like the Imitation Game—in which an impartial judge is to decide whether or not concealed Subject A and B are *really* female. The judge does this by posing leading questions to Subject A, a woman (who answers truthfully), and to Subject B, a man (who does his best to imitate a woman). The answers are returned in teletype to assure anonymity. The judge's questions are designed to reveal *who's zooming who*, while the Subject's answers are designed to fool the judge.

The Turing Test is logically identical to the Imitation Game, only instead of a *man and a woman*, we have a *person and a machine* (with the machine doing its best to imitate a person). It's worth pointing out, however, that the Turing Test is unquestionably limited. A machine *may never* experience its own sense of aliveness and awareness—yet, it may fool us into thinking otherwise.

Indeed, one could argue that the Turing Test is glaringly imperfect. For example, according to the rules of the Turing Test—even if a machine were to reach *dolphin-like* consciousness, it would still fail the test. Well, doesn't that seem a tad arbitrary? Isn't it rather chauvinistic and egocentric to assume that the only interesting type of consciousness is *human-like* consciousness? Perhaps. But notice the difficulties involved here. We take it on faith that *other people* experience things and perceive things (as an "I") just like we do. We don't *know* this with any certainty (perhaps *you're* in *my* dream, or, perhaps *I'm* in *your* dream, etc.). *And this deals with other humans.* Introducing a tricky subject like what a dolphin's consciousness might be like only takes us to the brick wall of inexplicability.

And so, the Turing Test wins by default. This inference-test is still the best determiner we have to go by to prove the presence of consciousness. We simply have no better way to determine the existence of an inner dialog.

A common misconception is that functionalism, although ostensibly materialistic, is in fact *dualistic*. The argument is that since any given mental state cannot be completely reduced to the particular mechanism that produces it, therefore mental states must be something more than the merely physical. There's a confusion here about "mental states" being necessarily identical regardless of the functional system from which they derive. Perhaps some straw-man functionalist would adhere to the principle that all mental states are identical regardless of the functional system from which they derive, but I sure don't. Every brain-like system, regardless of what it's made of, is going to be slightly different from others. Those differences *count*, at least in a fuzzy, probabilistic way. Rest assured, the brain-system of Einstein's is *different* from yours and mine.

The functionalist approach solves one of the classic problems recognized right at the start of psychology more than a hundred years ago. This is the homunculus problem. If we think of the eye as a camera, then it stands to reason that this camera sends a picture to our brain. Well, what in the brain looks at this picture? Perhaps another sort of "inner-eye"? Okay, maybe. But then how does this inner-eye see? Well, a picture is sent…and so on. This homunculus problem implies a little person, or homunculus, sitting in the brain looking at the pictures. The upshot is that either the homunculus has a kind of psychic eye to see with, or there is an infinite regress into a series of homunculi. Either way the problem of understanding perception becomes mysterious, if not infinitely regressive. Functionalism improves the picture significantly by removing the magic, and considering only the underlying processes involved.

Computers and humans currently do their tasks in completely different ways, but the underlying principles at work are remarkably similar. Consider how sophisticated information processing robots can interpret input-information from the outside environment so as to interact with the world. Granted, even the most sophisticated of these robots don't achieve near the level of complexity as a natural born squirrel, but still…A model or representation of the world is built by the input-information, and if that model is reasonably accurate enough, that sophisticated robot will be a "success" and perhaps be able to roam about (nonchalantly!) on the surface of Mars. Back on earth, the sophisticated robot walking around a room has to either be painstakingly programmed with the exact coordinates of the room or have the capacity to "learn" for itself a "make-do" representation of that room. Obviously, literal programming, whereby every conceivable variable possible in a given room is pre-set into the robot, is ultimately a hopeless undertaking. Unless, that is, you're really content to have the sophisticated robot be an absolute master when it comes to one room, but a complete moron anywhere else. No, whatever the programming might be, it had best be open-ended and adhere to the principle of A Variation on a Theme. Only then can the robot successfully move itself around, "learning" about its surroundings in a flexible and make-do manner. That's flexibility. That's the stuff of which survival requires. The contention here is that our brains have "learned" to build *good-enough* representations of the world over the make-do iterations of natural-selection's history, and that this is the skill that sophisticated robots must develop for them to survive and thrive in an unknown environment.

There are several different *types* of functionalism, one for every philosopher (oddly enough!). Most variations, however, are perhaps far too logically precise to be accurate. For functionalism to be interesting, it really has to exemplify a process capable of arising naturally and blindly from natural selection. It has to be *messy* and workable in a make-do sort of way. As evidence for this, consider once again how our perceptual system can be fooled by optical illusions. Whatever system underlies our consciousness, it must undoubtedly be just as imperfect.

An astute reader will know that the discussion so far presents no new ideas. Some readers may even be bored by the story so far. However, allow me to reiterate that in many ways I'm simply telling a story, and that a certain amount of narration is required before any truly satisfying conclusion can be possible. In other words, if one were to watch only the last ten minutes of, say, *The Sixth Sense*, whatever impact and significance the movie might otherwise contain would be entirely lost to that viewer because he or she would lack the appropriate context for the conclusion. And so I'm now asking the reader to hang in there. It's just that an appropriate context needs to be built up before I can present *any* conclusion that you'd find even the least bit satisfying.

Functionalism interprets consciousness in terms of *processes* rather than mere content. It attempts to explain consciousness via the messy computations underlying consciousness without explaining what it's like to have those experiences that the messy computations produce. There's a certain irony in this, and perhaps it's insurmountable. But really both sides are of equal importance: the function as well as the experience. One can have an intellectual understanding of "paralysis by analysis" but it's another thing entirely to be caught up in its web. I mean, seriously, can my being, my self, my life, my perceptions, my thoughts and beliefs, *really be fully described by a functionalist account?*

Physicist Roger Penrose in his books *The Emperor's New Mind* (1989) and *Shadows of the Mind* (1994) opposes functionalism, suggesting that a noncomputational element in nature is responsible for the development of consciousness. He differentiates between the *thinking process* which is computational and an *awareness of the thinking process* which he regards as noncomputational. His main argument in support of this assertion is Gödel's Theorem, which he feels displays a "human intuition" that is entirely impossible for a machine to mimic. On its face, this is dangerous waters—not all humans have the same amount of "intuition." Indeed, some are altogether *not-too-intuitive*. Does this fact count *against* Penrose's claim or *for* it? Conversely, some computer programs are more sophisticated than others. Is it really *impossible* for a suitably sophisticated program to exist that's capable of mimicking "human intuition"? If so, then wouldn't that make our brains that much more inexplicable and mysterious? Unless, that is, Penrose has some alternative to functionalism capable of ironing out all the wrinkles. Commendably, Penrose does provide a fragile guess—suggesting that conscious experience may be the result of quantum collapse in microtubules.

Many have scoffed at this association of consciousness with the quantum realm—implying that *just because both consciousness and the quantum realm are strange doesn't necessarily mean that the two are related*. Unfortunately for Penrose, even if we grant his argument, conscious experience remains utterly mystifying. Indeed, why should quantum processes in microtubules produce consciousness at all? How does isolating such a thing help explain "my" sense of *aliveness*, of *awareness*? After all, microtubules are found in almost *all* cells, not just neurons—does that mean our noses are conscious? Do they perhaps "cringe" when they sense a finger a-coming?

And really, isn't there just a basic contextual fallacy taking place here? Cars are explained on the level of carburetors and gas tanks, not on the level of quarks. Why should brains be any different?

The adoption of Penrose's position (and the resulting *denial* of process) basically makes the scientific study of consciousness an impossibility. Notice how a Penrosean scientist would be relegated to adopting a theory such as "conscious experience is the result of a quantum collapse in microtubules," and then never having a means to prove it! The only way to prove it would be for the scientist to get "outside of" his or her own awareness and experience the consciousness that the collapse of microtubules is said to produce. That's impossible, by definition. You can't even look at microtubule's behavior, let alone ask it a question or give it a Turing Test. There's absolutely no way of knowing whether or not microtubules have anything at all to do with consciousness! Isn't that remarkable?

So let's agree that Penrose's viewpoint can be likened to a brick wall, and that a Penrosean might be likened to a person that walks directly into that

brick wall. Penrose makes the study of consciousness impossible by definition, and his views are therefore difficult to accept. Note, however, that when it comes to consciousness we don't have much of a platform to stand on, so we are not in a position to out and out reject his notion. For the same exact reasons that Penrose's notion cannot be proven true, it also cannot be proven false. And this is not because Penrose is being deceptive. Rather, consciousness is just a subtle, surly unforgiving Beast.

Penrose is no dummy and we will be revisiting some of his supporting evidence for a noncomputational consciousness: specifically his arguments supporting a Platonic Realm, which are compelling,

Penrose's failure with microtubules doesn't mean we must "settle" for the computational theory just yet (after all, I *support* that theory, so we should certainly be very suspicious of it, *right*?!) After all, there is one other very influential argument against functionalism (the astute reader's eyes roll—*knowing* full well what I'm referring to…). This is known as the "Chinese Room." (Searle, 1980) So, before continuing with the computational theory of the mind, let's first make sure it can withstand the fury of the Chinese Room. Imagine yourself locked in a room given a task to hand-simulate an Artificial Intelligence (AI) program. The process is long and tedious. You (a non-Chinese speaking individual) are to mechanically decode various symbols and feed the decodings into the machine as results. The net effect is that the program passes the Turing Test and supposedly understands Chinese, while nobody in the room understands Chinese in the slightest.

While this argument is hardly decisive, it illustrates (arguably) how a machine can mechanically decode symbols without seeming to necessitate the slightest bit of awareness or understanding. The argument's weakness hinges upon *how* awareness actually emerges in nature. If awareness "pops up" blindly and stupidly in any and all occasions where a certain computational complexity has been achieved, then the Chinese Room becomes merely an example of *conceptual possibility*. Typically, critics of Searle's thought experiment are much harsher than this, and perhaps rightly so. Its non-technical qualities and easy story-telling manner has given the argument a life of its own: being retold countless times now. In the Chinese Room the human being so depicted would be equivalent to a *particular neuron* in our heads. We don't subscribe *awareness* to any particular neuron, only to the *system as a whole*. And, perhaps more to the point, Searle slows down the time-frame of the computation to such a crawl that even our own conscious manipulations would appear hackneyed and mechanistic at that speed (thus nullifying whatever point Searle was trying to make!). Internal brain processes are incredibly fast (at least relative to us) and reside on a level beneath our conscious understanding. By a similar tortuous turn we can string out 2 + 2 = 4 across the decades and suggest that there's no real "awareness" going on. Very trite. A meme that doesn't seem to ever go away.

Consider also the anti-functionalist sentiments by Nobel laureate neuroscientist Gerald Edelman. Edelman argues (in his book *Bright Air, Brilliant Fire*) that since computers carry out logical operations, computers are not a good example of thinking because "logic alone no more constitutes thinking than the physical events of adding up numbers on an abacus resemble what goes on in the brain during the performance or creation of arithmetic by a mathematician." And such an argument is undeniably true; at least relative to the strawman presented. Thinking is not *exactly* like a computer, rather a computer is *somewhat like* thinking. As of now, thinking is only seen in wet-ware (to borrow a Ruckerian phrase), and wet-ware is *not* a product of conscious design. *So it's not the same thing!* Furthermore, we'll probably never get to a robot-consciousness until we can forget pristine logic and figure out a way of patching the thing together in a *make-do* sort of way, or more succinctly, so that it might be a product of a natural selection among robots and the world of robots.

Edelman also notes how the symbols on a tape and how the states in a processor have the meaning assigned to them by a human programmer, and that without a human programmer to provide meaning to symbols, functionalism could never account for mind. The same argument was once made about perceived design in animals, and how an animal must have a designer just like a watch must have a designer. Why can't the symbols be patched together blindly by the Program of natural selection much like animals were patched together blindly by natural selection?

I believe that functionalism is really just an extension of the principles operating behind natural selection, incorporating very similar processes and really not adding anything astonishingly new to the picture. Inside that context, it makes it much easier to notice how question-begging some of Edelman's comments were. We're really talking about the same sorts of processes, and the only assumption being made is that if those processes can work for animals, then they can also work for brains. Functionalism and natural selection, when properly defined, are really the near-same process occurring in slightly different contexts. Such a consolidation of processes is greatly appealing in its elegance. It adheres to the principle of KISS—Keep It Simple Stupid.

We shouldn't arbitrarily add entirely distinct frameworks for each major phenomenon when we know that all frameworks must ultimately derive from the same big banged virtual particle. While this doesn't imply that frameworks for different phenomenon must be the same (as that would violate the principle of A Variation on a Theme), we should still expect a *similarity*. If we were to find that consciousness were best explained by something wholly different from anything else—so that it's not describable by any type of procedure, and so that it is not amenable to rational enquiry, then I think this would literally throw all of science and rationality in disarray.

Note that a functionalist account of consciousness is intrinsically saying that a brain is "like a computer." Well, it's not *really* a computer. Some even suggest, as does John Ratey in his *User's Guide to the Brain*:

> The brain is not a neatly organized system. It is often compared to an overgrown jungle of 100 billion nerve cells, or neurons, which begin as round cell bodies that grow processes called axons and dendrites. Each nerve cell has one axon and as many as 100,000 dendrites. Dendrites are the main way by which neurons get information (learn); and axons are the main way by which neurons pass on information to (teach) other neurons. The neuron and its thousands of neighbors send out roots and branches—the axons and dendrites—in all directions, which intertwine to form an interconnected tangle with 100 trillion constantly changing connections. There are more possible ways to connect the brain's neurons than there are atoms in the universe. The connections guide our bodies and behaviors, even as every thought and action we take physically modifies their patterns.

The jungle analogy might very well be more apt than a computer analogy. However, a jungle is literally "a jungle" and not compressible into an understandable model. Saying that something is like something else that is itself fantastically complicated and unknowable is not enlightening. In my view, both the brain and the jungle are best explained by the computer analogy. It's just that, in reality, there are thousands and thousands of separately manufactured "computers," each patched together for different selective functions, all working in parallel conjunction.

We strip away the *thousands* and focus on *one*, because at least that is somewhat understandable. A thousand computers is a *jungle*. One computer is a *model*. This is how science operates! This is how understanding works. Our minds are attracted to ideas that are elegant and simple. Just witness the popularity of the Right/Left brain distinction. It's based on fact, but boy how the generalizations have abounded! The reason for the popularity is because people absolutely *love* the simplicity and elegance involved in a brain that's half analytic, half romantic.

Science DOES NOT and CANNOT operate by viewing things to be an impenetrable jungle! We make an assumption about the brain's modulation, such that we assume different parts have different functions—each part acting as a sort of computer. For instance, the hippocampus is the part of the brain associated with memory. That association helps narrow the scope of inquiry. It simplifies things to help us understand otherwise utterly impenetrable processes. But scientists don't seriously believe that studying the hippocampus alone will tell us all there is to know about memory. There are many other factors involved, other parts of the brain also playing various roles. And Ratey knows this as well as anybody. That's why he aligns himself squarely with the standard position in all other respects, as reflected below:

> Neural Darwinism is the theory that explains why the brain needs to be plastic, that it's able to change as our environment and experiences change. That is why we can learn in the first place, and unlearn too, and why people with brain injuries can recover lost functions…"Neurons that fire together wire together" means that the more we repeat the same actions and thoughts—from practicing a tennis serve to memorizing multiplication tables—the more we encourage the formation of certain connections and the more fixed the neural circuits in the brain for that activity become. "Use it or lose it" is the corollary: if you don't exercise brain circuits, the connections will not be adaptive and will slowly weaken and could be lost.

The connections of neurons forming a circuit are rigid, yet flexible. Flexible enough to learn, and rigid enough to retain what was learned. The brain's plasticity does have limits, however, as any adult can testify who has ever tried learning a musical instrument, or a second language at the same time as his or her child. The child is in instinct stage, a sponge ready and willing to soak up *a lot* of what's fed to it, the circuits feverishly working to please the child (and of course the child is in no position to understand how remarkable any of this is!). To extend the analogy, the adult's brain can be likened to a sponge approaching the saturation point—it's much more difficult to soak anything up. The adult brain has lost some of its flexibility, and the going is rough. Age

makes it more difficult to reroute and establish new brain connections. The sage advice is to teach your children young.

"Circuit talk" is a drill-down of computer talk—functioning like the gates and wires in a computer, so the computer analogy stays. Besides, if the computer analogy were to be thrown out, we would have a lot of reconsidering to do. We would have to reconsider the big bang. We would have to reconsider natural selection. We would have to reconsider our entire rational enterprise. While, of course, some people *hate* science and *hate* western rationality, there's simply no need to throw everything away on account of consciousness. It's true that consciousness poses a remarkable puzzle in that we are forced to explain direct experience indirectly, but that is precisely what must be done. And we have to do it using the best analogy currently at our disposal; the computer.

The computer analogy is nothing new for those studying consciousness. Leda Cosmides and John Toody, Co-Directors of the Center for Evolutionary Psychology at the University of California, Santa Barbara, summarize their field this way in a 1994 brochure (Shermer, p.XXIII):

> Evolutionary psychology is based on the recognition that the human brain consists of a large collection of functionally specialized computational devices that evolved to solve the adaptive problems regularly encountered by our hunter-gatherer ancestors. Because humans share a universal evolved architecture, all ordinary individuals reliably develop a distinctively human set of preferences, motives, shared conceptual frameworks, emotion programs, content-specific reasoning procedures, and specialized interpretation systems—programs that operate beneath the surface of expressed cultural variability, and whose designs constitute a precise definition of human nature.

Let's switch our narrative a little here, and focus on how the general idea of functionalism handles *language*, in so far as language is a subset of consciousness.

BYTE EIGHT:

Language

http://www.philscanlan.net/

Say What?

"Before my teacher came to me, I did not know that I am. I lived in a world that was a no-world. I cannot hope to describe adequately that unconscious, yet conscious time of nothingness…Since I had no power of thought, I did not compare one mental state with another." This comes to us by way of Helen Keller. Very perceptively she uses language to say "unconscious, yet conscious" to denote that while language might not equate to consciousness outright, once you possess it, language sure changes everything!

Next to consciousness, *language* is perhaps that most pernicious of intellectual topics as it's *right there*—at the tip of our tongues—yet we have no real idea what it is or why it came to be. Indeed, what better evidence is there for something being conscious than having the ability to communicate in a *language*?

But do we even need words in order to think?

Probably not, but language certainly enhances and clarifies thinking. The only type of thinking entirely unaffected by language would be picture-images used in geometric problem-solving. So in that sense it's certainly true we can not only think but even think quite clearly without words (albeit sans speech and writing). It's just a potentially limited, restricted sort of thinking. Even so, it absolutely flies in the face of the conventional wisdom that *language determines the categories of thought*—that linguistics is relative. We remember factoids from school that claim *the Hopi concept of time is fundamentally different from ours*, and *Eskimo's have dozens of words for snow*. The implication for cultural relativity runs heavy with such talk. Yet, there's good reason to believe it entirely wrong. (Pinker, 1994)

All human societies have language. As far as we know they always did; language was not invented by some groups and spread to others like agriculture or the alphabet. All languages are complex computational systems employing the same basic kinds of rules and representations, with no notable correlation with technological progress: the grammars of industrial societies are no more complex than the grammars of hunter-gatherers; Modern English is not an advance over Old English. Within societies, individual humans are proficient language users regardless of intelligence, social status, or level of education. Children are fluent speakers of complex grammatical sentences by the age of three, without benefit of formal instruction. They are capable of inventing languages that are more systematic than those they hear, showing resemblances to languages that they have never heard, and they obey subtle grammatical principles for which there is no evidence in their environments. Disease or injury can make people linguistic savants while severely retarded, or linguistically impaired with normal intelligence. Some language disorders are genetically transmitted. Aspects of language skill can be linked to characteristic regions of the human brain. The human vocal tract is tailored to the demands of speech, compromising other functions such as breathing and swallowing. Human auditory perception shows complementary specializations toward the demands of decoding speech sounds into linguistic segments.

This list of facts (see Pinker, 1989) suggests that the ability to use a natural language belongs more to the study of human biology than human culture; it is a topic like echolocation in bats or stereopsis in monkeys, not like writing or the wheel. All modern students of language agree that at least some aspects of language are due to species-specific, task-specific biological abilities, though of course there are radical disagreements about those specifics. A prominent position, outlined by Chomsky (1965, 1980, 1981, 1986, 1988), Fodor (1983), Lenneberg (1964, 1967), and Liberman (Liberman, Cooper, Shankweiler, & Studdert-Kennedy, 1967; Liberman and Mattingly, 1989), is that the mind is composed of autonomous computational modules and that the acquisition and representation of language is the product of several such specialized modules. This contrasts with the theory of language that identifies thought with words, and identifies different words found in different languages with cultural relativism.

Linguist Steven Pinker, in his *The Language Instinct*, argues very effectively that the anthropological anecdotes such assertions rely on are "bunk." Typically, the conclusions are drawn from shoddy research and obvious *preconceptions*. Pinker notes that linguist Benjamin Lee Worf did not study any Apaches, and probably never even met one. Yet, he managed to render their sentences in clumsy, word-for-word translations, even when a much simpler interpretation was possible (like Pinker's example of "Clear stuff—water—is falling" as opposed to Worf's convenient rendering of the same phrase into unintelligible nonsense for the purpose, one supposes, of better getting his point across). Much the same way, the mundane English sentence "He walks" can be rendered "As solitary masculinity, leggedness proceeds." (Pinker, 1995)

Even so, it's still possible that the anthropological anecdotes, *although baseless as anecdotes*, are still founded upon a correct interpretation of how language actually works (namely, that *language determines the categories of our thought*). However, the controlled studies of the past thirty-five years, testing even the "weak" versions of the Whorfian hypothesis that language is in some sense the sole master of our thought, have continually met with failure. On the other hand, there are *too many* examples of a more fundamental *mentalese* to suggest something otherwise—examples of which include any and all of the following:

- Pinker: "Many creative people insist that in their most inspired moments they think not in words but in mental images. Samuel Taylor Coleridge wrote that visual images of scenes and words once appeared involuntarily before him in a dreamlike state (perhaps opium-induced). He managed to copy the first forty lines onto paper, resulting in the poem we know as "Kubla Khan," before a knock on the door shattered the images and obliterated forever what would have been the rest of the poem. Many contemporary novelists, like Joan Didion, report that their acts of creation begin not with any notion of a character or a plot but with vivid mental pictures that dictate their choice of words. The modern sculptor James Surls plans his projects lying on a couch listening to music; he manipulates the sculptures in his mind's eye, he says, putting an arm on, taking an arm off, watching the images roll and tumble. Physical scientists are even more adamant that their thinking is geometrical, not verbal. Michael Faraday, the originator of our modern conception of electric and magnetic fields, had no training in mathematics but arrived at his insights by visualizing lines of force as narrow tubes curving through space. James Clerk Maxwell formalized the concepts of electromagnetic fields in a set of mathematical equations and is considered the prime example of an abstract theoretician, but he set down the equations only after mentally playing the elaborate imaginary models of sheets and fluids. Nikola Tesla's idea for the electrical motor and generator, Friedrich Kekulé's discovery of the benzene ring that kicked off modern organic chemistry, Ernest Lawrence's conception of the cyclotron, James Watson and Francis Crick's discovery of the DNA double helix—all came to them in images." (Pinker, 1995)

- Albert Einstein: "the words or the language, as they are written or spoken, do not seem to play any role in my mechanism of thought. The psychical entities which seem to serve as elements of thought are certain signs and more or less clear images which can be "voluntarily" reproduced and combined...The above mentioned elements are, in my case, of visual and some muscular type. Conventional words or other signs have to be sought for laboriously only in a second stage, when the mentioned associative play is sufficiently established and can be reproduced at will." (Penrose, 1989)

- Geneticist Francis Galton: "It is a serious drawback to me in writing, and still more in explaining myself, that I do not think as easily in words as otherwise. It often happens that after being hard at work, and having arrived at results that are perfectly clear and satisfactory to myself, when I try to express them in language I feel that I must begin by putting myself upon quite another intellectual plane. I have to translate my thoughts into a language that does not run very evenly with them. I therefore waste a vast deal of time in seeking appropriate words and phrases, and am conscious, when required to speak on a sudden, of being often very obscure through mere verbal maladroitness, and not through want of clearness of perception. That is one of the small annoyances of my life." (Penrose, 1989)

- Philosopher Bryan Magee: "If I look up from the writing of this sentence, my view immediately takes in half a room containing scores if not hundreds of multicolored items and shapes in higgledy-piggledy relationships with one another. I see it all clearly and distinctly, instantly and effortlessly. There is no conceivable form of words into which this simple, unitary act of vision can be put. For most of my waking day my conscious awareness is a predominantly visual experience—as Fichte puts it, "I am a living seeing"—but there are no words to describe the irregular shapes of most of the objects I see, nor are there any words to describe the multiple, coexisting three-dimensional spatial relationships in which I directly see them as standing to one another. There are no words for the multifarious densities of light and shadow. *Whenever*

I see, all that language can do is to indicate with the utmost generality and in the broadest and crudest of terms what it is that I see. Even something as simple and everyday as the sight of a towel dropped on to the bathroom floor is inaccessible to language—and inaccessible to it from many points of view at the same time: no words to describe the shape it has fallen into, no words to describe the degrees of shading in its colours, no words to describe the differentials of shadow in its folds, no words to describe its spatial relationships to all the other objects in the bathroom. I see all these things at once with great precision and definiteness, with clarity and certainty, and in all their complexity. I possess them all wholly and securely in direct experience, and yet I would be totally unable, as would anyone else, to put that experience into words. It is emphatically not the case, then, that "the world is the world as we describe it," or that I "experience it through linguistic categories that help to shape the experiences themselves" or that my "main way of dividing things up is in language" or that my "concept of reality is a matter of our linguist categories." (Magee, 1997)

- Picture an "F" rotating slowly in your mind. No language is required to do that.

- Most stroke victims lose their ability of speech communication (both verbal and written), even though they remain "alert, attentive and fully aware of where he was and why he was there." (Pinker, 1995) Their grammatical impairment apparently does not effect their ability to think. In fact, their Intelligence Quotient in nonverbal areas could stay in the high-average range.

All these examples attest to a basic computational thinking ability that we have. I take it as obvious that without language, thinking would be a pretty boring affair, apparently limited to "picture-images" and "searching for something that you don't know what you're searching for." Nevertheless, the examples given refute the contention that language itself rules thought. The examples provide ample enough evidence that thought exists at a more basic and fundamental level than language. Language helps shape an otherwise unfocused structure such that much more constructive thinking can be accomplished with a human brain that possesses language than without.

Instincts

We all know animals have instincts and there have been many experiments over the years that illustrate just how "blind" these behaviors really are. One instinctual response among gulls, geese, and other ground-nesting birds, for example, is to reach over and roll back an egg—with the underside of its bill—that has rolled out of the nest. This process is blind. It has been demonstrated (Tinbergen) that gulls will perform the same action even when the "gull eggs" are actually hens" eggs, wooden cylinders, or cocoa tins. (Dawkins, 1995) Sometimes this blindness leads to tragedy. In this regard, turkey mothers have an instinctual method of defending their young; namely, attack anything that moves near the nest, unless it makes a baby-turkey noise. (Schleidt) On one occasion, the mother killed off all her babies. Was she a bad mother? Probably not. She was simply deaf. (Dawkins, 1995)

A similar tragedy can easily befall the bee, which gives off oleic acid when it finds itself decaying as a corpse. The smell of oleic acid produces in the living bees a conditioned response whereby the dead body is removed from the hive. Well, paint a live bee with oleic acid and guess what happens? Yup, it will be dragged off kicking and screaming, and left with the dead. (Dawkins, 1995)

Another insect example concerns the wasp. A digger wasp returns to her burrow with paralyzed prey in tow. Her instinct is to leave the prey outside, enter the burrow—apparently to verify that all is well—and then drag the prey in. An experimenter can move the prey a few inches from where it was left, and the wasp will be forced to relocate the prey and reposition it in front of the burrow. Then, the wasp will blindly reenter the burrow and repeat the procedure that had just been performed. At this point, the experimenter can move the prey once again, inspiring the same responses from the wasp. This process can be repeated *ad infinitum*. (Dawkins, 1995)

Likewise, we *instinctually* know the meaningfulness of a sentence. Consider how *Last night I slept bad dreams a hangover snoring no pajamas sheets were wrinkled* seems so obviously out of order. (Pinker, 1995) Well, why, precisely, does it seem that way? *Because language is an instinct.* Typically, such a bald assertion conjures up a negative knee-jerk response. Some, for example, may claim that a language-instinct is anti-evolutionary. After all, no other animal even comes close in our language abilities. If it was instinctual, shouldn't there be a steady gradation of language throughout our evolutionary branch?

We might be descendants of the apes, yet no non-human ape has the ability to communicate in a language. Chimpanzees, supposedly the second-best learners in the animal kingdom (perhaps dolphins hold a better claim to this title), are a *very* distant second at that. Shouldn't chimpanzees be able to acquire a language? Assuming an overly-simplistic brand of natural selection, it seems quite obvious that they should. But they can't.

The findings on chimp-research, although heavily promoted in the mass media, are very scant in actual evidence. While chimpanzees can learn to dress, use the toilet, brush their teeth, and wash the dishes, their behavioral mimicry seems *limited* to such reward-based demonstrations. (Pinker, 1995) A chimpanzee cannot *speak* any more than can a dog, and while some charitable listeners may claim to hear certain words here and there, such anecdotal evidence is not the stuff of which science is made. Their inability to communicate by voice, however, tells us very little. After all, they are *not* physically equipped with the same voice-apparatus that we possess. In other words, since they don't have the exact-same machine-parts that we have, perhaps expecting them to speak *just like us* is a bit far-fetched. Notice, however, that this limitation does *not* apply to American Sign Language. So then, shouldn't a baby chimp be able to learn American Sign Language?

Indeed, experiments *have been* done on this, and the results *have been* trumpeted. Washoe and Koko (a chimp and a gorilla, respectively) were said to have *learned* American Sign Language. Koko's trainer even claimed that "language is no longer the exclusive domain of man." (Pinker, 1995) Heady talk. As might be expected, the mass media and the popular pundits jumped on this claim; some even suggesting that this was among the *scientific discoveries of the century*. For did it not *prove* natural selection? Did it not *vindicate* gradualism?

The actual evidence for the acquisition of language by chimps amounts to little more than aunt Bella claiming that her Siamese cat "Rusty" understands English. (Pinker, 1995) The trainers excuse poor performance and an inability to reproduce results by claiming that the animal enjoys puns, jokes, and mischievous lies. (Pinker, 1995) These are spurious claims indeed. Spoon-benders have trouble reproducing their miracles under controlled conditions as well. One of their excuses for poor performance is that the straight-jacket of scientific experiment hampers the *creative spirit*. The point? Excuses can always be made, but excuses should not be confused with actual evidence.

The apes never learned American Sign Language. As Pinker wrote,

> This preposterous claim is based on the myth that ASL is a crude system of pantomimes and gestures rather than a full language with complex phonology, morphology, and syntax. In fact the apes did

not learn *any* true ASL signs. The one deaf native signer on the Washoe team later made these candid remarks:

"Every time the chimp made a sign, we were supposed to write it down in the log…. They were always complaining because my log didn't show enough signs. All the hearing people turned in logs with long lists of signs. They always saw more signs than I did…I watched really carefully. The chimp's hands were moving constantly. Maybe I missed something, but I don't think so. I just wasn't seeing any signs. The hearing people were logging every movement the chimp made as a sign. Every time the chimp put his finger in his mouth, they'd say "Oh, he's making the sign for *drink*," and they'd give him some milk…. When the chimp scratched itself, they'd record it as the sign for *scratch*…. When [the chimps] want something, they reach. Sometimes [the trainers would] say, "Oh, amazing, look at that, it's exactly like the ASL sign for give!" It wasn't." (Pinker, 1995)

Boy, what's the signer's *problem*? Perhaps the great assumptions involved hadn't quite *sunk in* yet. Perhaps the signer failed to understand the lofty dichotomy of *God or Natural Selection*. Didn't the signer understand that "natural selection" means gradualism, and *that's that*, end of discussion? Apparently, the signer wasn't *educated enough* to be involved in such "scientific" work.

The upshot? While performing experiments on chimps smacks of science, over-bloated claims and unsupportable "results" smacks of something else entirely.

So then, language is basically unique to humans. But doesn't this uniqueness imply that it could not have developed through natural selection? Sure, and I suppose that the same can be said for an elephant's trunk, or a giraffe's long neck. In truth, there are many different species that have unique characteristics. It's not at all clear that those unique characteristics are *fully determined* by the principle of *survival*. Or should we assert that an elephant's trunk or a giraffe's neck **needs** to be *just that long*?

The very suggestion is usually the result of *not quite having thought these things through*. Consider the assumptions underlying the following remark by Chomsky-critic Elizabeth Bates:

If the basic structural principles of language cannot be learned (bottom up) or derived (top down), there are only two possible explanations for their existence: either Universal Grammar was endowed to us directly by the Creator, or else our species has undergone a mutation of unprecedented magnitude, a cognitive equivalent of the big bang.... We have to abandon any strong version of the discontinuity claim that has characterized generative grammar for thirty years. We have to find some way to ground symbols and syntax in the mental material that we share with other species.

Oh, I see now. "Either, Or." Just accept this false, overly-simplistic argument and then all is well. **Either** there's God, **Or** there's Chance. End of discussion. And what of evolution? Shouldn't evolution be viewed as *a linear tree*—a gradual, resourceful progression toward whatever characteristics we possess? From amoebas to frogs to chimps to humans? Ah, that must be it. There's a well-known factoid that chimpanzees and humans share 98% to 99% of their DNA. Therefore we must be 99% similar, right? Case solved!

Not so fast, consider what Pinker has to say about this:

...[G]eneticists are appalled at such reasoning and take pains to stifle it in the same breath that they report their results. The recipe for the embryological soufflé is so baroque that small genetic changes can have enormous effects on the final product. And a 1% difference is not even so small. In terms of the information content in the DNA it is 10 megabytes, big enough for Universal Grammar with lots of room left over for the rest of the instructions on how to turn a chimp into a human. Indeed, a 1% difference in total DNA does not even mean that only 1% of human and chimpanzee genes are different. It could, in theory, mean that 100% of human and chimpanzee genes are different, each by 1%. DNA is a discrete combinatorial code, so a 1% difference in the DNA for a gene can be as significant as a 100% difference, just as changing one bit in every byte, or one letter in every word, can result in a new text that is 100% different, not 10% or 20% different.

Pinker doesn't agree with the linear picture of evolution, preferring the picture of a nonlinear bush instead. While I like Pinker's picture, it all melts together best under A Variation on a Theme. First, there's an algorithm *that cannot not be* (the Theme). Next, the *possibility of a possibility* being thus established, there's a space-time Variation—an algorithmic belch. By default, natural selection propels this

belch. By default, the whims of natural selection are limited by the Theme being varied.

This is all well and good. Yet, how do *we* learn language? How is such a thing even possible?

Language-learning

The *learning* of a language also puts paid to its innateness. Consider how mysterious the very process of learning a language is. Let's say that a child hears *gavagai*, or any other word (it doesn't really matter) and that the word is usually associated by a shout—so that when a rabbit scurries by, the word "gavagai" is typically exclaimed. Yet, **must** the word mean *rabbit*?

> It could mean any furry thing, any mammal, or any member of that species of rabbit (say, *Oryctolagus cuniculus*), or any member of that variety of that species (say chinchilla rabbit). It could mean scurrying rabbit, rabbit plus the ground it scurries upon, or scurrying in general. It could mean footprint-maker, or habitat for rabbit-fleas. It could mean the top half of a rabbit, or rabbit-meat-on-the-hoof, or possessor of at least one rabbit's foot. It could mean anything that is either a rabbit or a Buick. It could mean collection of undetached rabbit parts, or "Lo! Rabbithood again!," or "It rabbiteth," analogous to "It raineth."

> The problem is the same when the child is the linguist and the parents are the natives. Somehow a baby must intuit the correct meaning of a word and avoid the mind-boggling number of logically impeccable alternatives. It is an example of a more general problem that Quine calls "the scandal of induction," which applies to scientists and children alike: how can they be so successful at observing a finite set of events and making some correct generalization about all future events of that sort, rejecting an infinite number of false generalizations that are also consistent with the original observations? (Pinker, 1995)

While some theorists, like Chomsky, will readily claim this as further evidence for the innateness of language, other theorists, like the Swiss psychologist Jean

Piaget, want to deny innateness outright. Piaget's idea was that language was merely a subset to a more general problem-solving ability possessed by humans.

> Although Piaget's approach rings true with regard to many aspects of our early learning experience, the acquisition of linguistic skills confronts it with a number of striking facts that Chomsky used to support his view that language is an inbuilt instinct.
>
> Although children are exposed to the structure of language—its syntax and grammar—only at a superficial level, they are able to carry out many complicated abstract constructions. The average five-year-old's exposure to language is insufficient to explain his or her linguistic proficiency. Children can use and understand sentences that they have never heard before. No matter how poor they may be at other activities, able-bodied children never fail to learn to speak. This expertise is achieved without specific instruction. The amount of environmental interaction that they experience is insufficient to explain their linguistic proficiency. Children seem to develop linguistic proficiency most rapidly between the ages of two and three irrespective of their exposure levels. Attempts to learn foreign languages by older individuals do not meet with the same success, nor do adults respond to the same educational process. The sponge-like learning ability of a child appears to turn off at an early age. (Barrow, 1995)

At issue is whether or not humans were capable of inventing their own language. While the very idea may initially seem incoherent, I'm willing to bet that many support it simply because they believe in that Great Dichotomy—*If language was not invented, then it must have been designed; it couldn't have been designed, ergo, it must have been invented.* However, such thinking is sloppy and overly-simplistic.

Language as Computation

Chomsky suggests that we are born with super-rules that are universal and innate. When children learn a particular language, they don't have to learn a long list of rules because they are born with the super-rules.

All they have to learn is whether their particular language has the parameter value head-first, as in English, or head-last, as in Japanese. They can do that merely by noticing whether a verb comes before or after its object in any sentence in their parents" speech. If the verb comes before the object, as in Eat your spinach!, the child concludes that the language is head-first; if it comes after, as in Your spinach eat!, the child concludes that the language is head-last. Huge chunks of grammar are then available to the child, all at once, as if the child were merely flipping a switch to one of two possible positions. (Pinker, 1995)

[C]onsider a specific example of this computational device with which we are born. Occasionally, new words and phrases are born in our language—for example, *Walkman* and *fly-out* (in the baseball sense). The computational rules are as such that the plural of *Walkman* is *Walkmans* (not *Walkmen*), and the past-tense of a *fly-out* is *flied out* (not *flown out*). Here's why:

The real rationale for flied out and Walkmans comes from the algorithm for interpreting the meanings of complex words from the meanings of the simple words they are built out of. [W]hen a big word is built out of smaller words, the big word gets all its properties from one special word sitting inside it at the extreme right: the head. The head of the verb *to overshoot* is the verb *to shoot*, so *overshooting* is a kind of *shooting*, and it is a verb, because *shoot* is a verb. Similarly, a *workman* is a singular noun, because *man*, its head, is a singular noun, and it refers to a kind of man, not a kind of work.

...The source of quirkiness in words like *fly-out* and *Walkmans* is their *headlessness*. A headless word is an exceptional item that, for one reason or another, differs in some property from its rightmost element, the one it would be based on if it were like ordinary words. A simple example of a headless word is a *low-life*—not a kind of life at all but a kind of person, namely one who leads a low life. In the word *low-life*, then, the normal percolation pipeline must be blocked. Now, a pipeline inside a word cannot be blocked for just one kind of information; if it is blocked for one thing, nothing passes through. If *low-life* does not get its meaning from life, it cannot get its plural from life either. The irregular form associated with *life*, namely *lives*, is trapped in the dictionary, with no way to bubble up to the whole word *low-life*. The all-purpose regular rule, "Add the -s suffix," steps in by default, and we get *low-lifes*. By similar unconscious reasoning, speakers arrive at *saber-tooths* (a kind of tiger, not a kind of tooth), *tenderfoots* (novice cub scouts who are not a kind of foot but a kind of youngster that has tender feet), *flatfoots* (also not a kind of foot but a slang term for policemen), and *still lifes* (not a kind of life but a kind of painting). (Pinker, 1995)

While more can be said in regards to the computation of language, I think the case is sufficiently made so that the reader has a general idea as to what the argument is. My goal is not to *prove* that language is computational (although I'm not sure what else it could possibly be) as I don't think science has as yet reached the point of making such a thing provable. Rather, the goal is simply to communicate an idea, an analogy, *a way of looking at things* that seems useful and relevant. Admittedly, I have done little here aside from regurgitating the views of Chomsky and particularly Pinker.

The truth of the matter is that while language is important and deserves a summary discussion, I don't consider it part of my main argument so I honestly don't have any unique insights to add to the mix. Generically, I suppose that the computational process behind language can best be explained by means of A Variation on a Theme. *The work of Chomsky and Pinker suggests that the thought-process underlying language is computational in form.* How could such a thing be? Because our innate ability of thought-processing is simply A Variation on a Theme—a Theme that *cannot not be*, and which is, at its very core, an algorithmic paradox. While A Variation on a Theme certainly does not *explain* our possession of language anymore than it might explain an elephant's possession of a trunk, it might very well provide a thematic basis for potentiality. I think there's a real difficulty in understanding how things like language are intrinsically possible in the first place; how is it even *possible* that such a thing can exist. If nothing else, A Variation on a Theme proposes that an algorithmic process is the thematic root of all variations such that its assumed characteristic of unconscious experience provides the basis for the variations we see in this world and that we ourselves possess. Whether we want to call the algorithmic folk-conclusion of "I am" a *language* or some sort of *mentalese*, I think a somewhat persuasive argument can be made that A Variation on a Theme provides the Theme for our language being a particular type of *mutated/accidental* Variation of the initial Conflict (the symbolic "1

&/or Ø"). While the Theme did not possess "language" *per se*, neither did it possess "ten toes." Likewise, an amoeba does not possess hands to hold a cane nor a head to rest a hat, yet somehow we managed to evolve from such a thing. To put it bluntly, Variation by algorithmic process is a very powerful concept.

BYTE NINE:

UNCONSCIOUS EXPERIENCE

http://www.philscanlan.net/

The Human Noodle

All mammals, birds, reptiles, fish, and amphibians have brains. If they didn't, they would not be alive. Brains give rise to *experience* and without experience there cannot be *life*. Despite this commonality among animals, human brains are unique in how they give us the power to think, plan, speak, and imagine in a way not seen in any other animal. What gives?

Well, I believe that question is rationally unanswerable. Our brains are a evolutionary product of haphazard events. We'll be returning to this idea again during the Wrap-Up, but for now let's just focus on the brain itself.

The brain performs many important tasks: controlling our body temperature, blood pressure, heart rate and breathing; accepting a flood of information about the world around us from our various senses (eyes, ears, nose, etc.); handling physical motion when walking, talking, standing or sitting; and letting us think, dream, reason and experience emotions.

These life-essential tasks are all coordinated, controlled and regulated by an organ that is about the size of a small head of cauliflower: our respective brains.

Our brains are made up of approximately 100-billion nerve cells, called neurons. Neurons gather and transmit electrochemical signals, passing messages to each other—functioning like the gates and wires in a computer. Even the simplest of creatures have rudimentary nervous systems made up of nothing but reflex pathways. While creatures like flatworms and invertebrates do not have a centralized brain, they yet possess loose associations of neurons that link together to form a "neural net" around the entire animal. Slightly more complex creatures have evolved nervous systems that transform into rudimentary brains. Lower animals like fish, reptiles, and birds concern themselves with the everyday business of gathering food, eating, drinking, sleeping, reproducing and defending themselves. And their brains are a reflection of what they do.

We perform these functions as well, and so we also have a "reptilian" brain built into us—a lower-level platform from which add-ons have been patched. Significantly, this lower-level platform is found in all brains, consisting of the Brain Stem (controls the reflexes and automatic functions of the heart rate and blood pressure), the Cerebellum (helps in the coordination of limb movement), and the Hypothalamus and Pituitary Gland (controls body temperature and the behavioral responses of feeding, drinking, aggression, pleasure,

and the sexual impulse). Tellingly, during the development of the human embryo a chronological "movie" is played showing the evolution from lizard to human. We're a patch-worked system.

A key add-on for higher-level brains is the Cerebrum, which integrates information from all the sense organs. It controls emotions and holds memory and thought processes, and also happens to be the largest part of the human brain. Such an add-on may be little more than a useful by-product of something else that was selected for a completely different purpose. For example, a nose evolved for smelling and warming and moistening air but can also be used for wearing spectacles. Likewise, our brains may possess functions that were never directly selected for in nature. And it's VERY important to understand that such a non-selective possibility introduces an intrinsic nonlinearity to natural selection, that while unavoidable is also unwelcome. It means that *understanding* selective processes becomes a virtually meaningless term: because many characteristics and functions later found most important might never have been directly selected in the first place (putting the entire "reverse engineering" enterprise on very shaky footing).

Unconscious Experience

The major problem confronting us when we contemplate consciousness is that it's a sprawling, complex, undefinable mess. There's self-awareness, feelings, emotions, language, a more basic phenomenal or experiential consciousness, intention, intelligence, perception, unconscious processes, and on and on it goes. Couple this with the mind-numbing fact that no other animal, having gone through the same evolutionary program we went through, came out the other end exhibiting human-like consciousness. The possibility, becoming more and more obvious, is that human-like consciousness might be flat-out unexplainable, in that it's a freak occurrence in much the same way that an elephant's trunk is literally unexplainable. It's quite easy to formulate Just-So speculations that could account for an elephant's trunk, but I'm looking for a more definitive answer to the question—how was it that humans came to possess consciousness add-ons while other animals have not?

One way of explaining this is with the following reasoning: Perhaps there's a very basic program of "experience" that is common to all life, a fundamental property of all living things. Additional programs are then tacked onto this initial program over the course of meandering natural selection. In this manner of thinking, looking at the most primitive examples of life could theoretically be rewarding. If there really is a commonality of experience among life forms, much like there is a commonality in brain structures among life forms (such that human brains have a lower-level brain stem common to all animals possessing higher-order add-ons)—then it seems a "no-brainer" that understanding basic experience in lower animals would tell us something meaningful that applies to all of life (and not just humans!). A single-celled amoeba "hunting" for food and responding to various stimuli, in its natural environment of the mud found in freshwater streams and ponds, might tell us something basic about ourselves—albeit in a very abstract way.

Well, this idea is not new and has indeed been pursued before, and the problem it poses is unavoidable and insurmountable. We can't get inside an amoeba to determine if it actually experiences anything, or if it just mechanically proceeds from one chemical reaction to another.

Much of modern-day neurological research is human-biased. And the simple and undeniable reason for this is that we can't be sure that other animals have an inner representation, an inner "dialog" (a mentalese) or just flat-out any kind of *experience* as we do. The nature of human consciousness is such that "I" can only be certain about my own inner dialog, as there is no direct access into anybody else's inner dialog. So "I" am forced to infer that other humans have an "I" as well. This is undoubtedly a safe assumption, but it is important to note our inability to directly verify this most fundamental of human qualities. This fuzziness only compounds itself once we leave the human realm, let alone try to explore "experiences" at the boundaries of life.

Our human-like consciousness and our language are probably freak occurrences, and yet because we are the benefactors of such freak occurrences, we have literally no other choice but to use our freakish selves as the standard-bearers. Yet our peculiar sense of "self" and our use of language are probably unexplainable in and of themselves and need to be considered as "add-on's" to a more fundamental experience.

We could theoretically map, accurately and definitively, all the parts of all the brains in all the world; have a complete wiring diagram of all the nervous systems for each organism that has ever existed; know everything there is to know about brainworks; and still never, not EVER, know on the basis of all that knowledge which brains and nervous systems possess experience and which ones don't. That fundamental distinction between the thing that experiences and the things that are experienced is a Brick Wall. Forget our use of language, our "inner dialogs" and our other higher-order forms of human thought. Most of the processes are unconscious anyway.

Our sense of "self-awareness" may well be a fluky byproduct of language which itself may be a fluky byproduct of a patched-together brain that had flukily grown much bigger than ever needed. How can we learn from such a fluky end-product? How can we compare it to anything else?

Paleontologist Stephen J. Gould illustrated the possibility of our self-awareness being a richly meaningless accident brilliantly by developing a theory centered around two new terms he introduced to his field: *exaptation* and *spandrel*. Rudimentary inquiries into natural selection suggest that a trait develops because it helps an animal survive. Case closed. But times and environments change. Niches change. What happens to that animal and its trait when the conditions that led to the initial trait have changed? Well, sometimes a trait that was originally used in one way comes in handy enough to make-do in some other situation. In Gould's terminology, a trait originally used one way is *exapted* into another use. Sometimes a foreleg originally used for walking is exapted into a wing that's used for an entirely different purpose than originally programmed. Sometimes a furry proto-feather originally used to keep warm is exapted into feathers used for flight.

Meanwhile, a *spandrel* is an architectural term referring to something that exists only as a consequence of something else. An example is the vertical boards between steps in a staircase. They serve no function in themselves, and have no structural import. It's just a "hole" that needs to be filled. In evolutionary terms, a spandrel is a trait that exists not because it has selective advantage for the animal, but because it must exist as a consequence of some other trait. A commonly cited example is that of the male nipple. Male nipples are useless, neither providing an advantage nor disadvantage to the male animal. Males have them because females have them, and because it was evidently easier for the Program of Life to develop a single "proto-nipple" for both sexes, only "turning on" in one of the sexes.

So our complexity, even our most ballyhooed characteristic of consciousness, might be *meaningless*. However, I believe that in this world, even in the midst of meaninglessness, we find a bedrock of certainty. Re-consider *experience*. Specifically, *unconscious experience*.

Might unconscious experience be an essential quality of life (whether it can ever be scientifically proven or not)? What even is such a thing as "unconscious experience"? How could we even know of such a thing seeing how we can't consciously experience it?

Perhaps we really do get occasional glimpses of what this might be like, but it's just hard to detect. Consider a time when you were playing tennis (or whatever it is that you truly love doing), and you sort of "lost" yourself for a period of time in that occupation. Time elapsed, but you were so absorbed in whatever it was that you were doing that you literally were not conscious of time passing. Is it really a stretch to suggest that in such situations we are literally unconscious? We didn't black-out, go comatose, and our system didn't collapse. We retained the *experience* of that moment, yet we may not have been conscious of that moment. Typically, it's when our self-awareness becomes involved that we get in trouble—as in a game of tennis, it's when we start worrying about our "form" that our game rapidly deteriorates in spite of our best conscious efforts for it not to. Paradoxically, we function at our best with low-level *experience*, leaving higher-order *self-awareness* out of the picture.

To paint the scene a bit, I think we're all familiar with the fact that our conscious minds do not control our basic bodily functions. We do not consciously command ourselves to breathe, swallow, blink, digest, and so on. Occasionally, we can consciously control our breathing, swallowing, or blinking for a short time, but for the most part they are controlled by processes operating behind the scenes.

We are also somewhat familiar with the relative ease, the instinctual, unconscious ease that a child has in learning his native language. Later, when we try to consciously learn a second language we have a much tougher go at it (although we might still find success). Also, we are familiar with the years of practice that a concert pianist might need to reach the heights of his profession. We also might be familiar with the paradoxical notion that a pianist does not consciously think about what he's doing in the middle of a recital. If he consciously did think about the meticulous movements of his fingers upon each respective key in each respective lapse of time, his performance would be an utter disaster.

From personal experience, we are also familiar with the phenomenon of driving a familiar route (like to and from work) while not being particularly conscious of the act of driving. The act of driving becomes a mechanical function that at times seems to not even register in our awareness. Consider the following from Julian Jaynes *The Origin of Consciousness in the Breakdown of the Bicameral Mind* (the first 70 or so pages of which I recommend as highly as anything can be recommended):

Does the door of your room open from the right or the left? Which is your second longest finger? At a stoplight, is it the red or the green that is on top? How many teeth do you see when brushing your teeth? What letters are associated with what numbers on a telephone dial? If you are in a familiar room, without turning around, write down all the items on the wall just behind you, and then look.

I think you will be surprised how little you can retrospect in consciousness on the supposed images you have stored from so much previous attentive experience. If the familiar door suddenly opened the other way, if another finger suddenly grew longer, if the red light were differently placed, or you had an extra tooth, or the telephone were made differently, or a new window latch had been put on the window behind you, you would know it immediately, showing that you all along "knew," but not consciously so. Familiar to psychologists, this is the distinction between recognition and recall. What you can consciously recall is a thimbleful to the huge oceans of your actual knowledge.

Of course, it kind of begs the question how someone can possess knowledge of something that they are incapable of consciously recalling, but you get the drift. There's a lot of common-place "facts" that never enter our conscious awareness that were they to suddenly change would yet be noticed for having changed. Unconscious processes; our ghost in the machine. Note that the phrase of "ghost in the machine" is not being used here in its original sense of ridiculing dualism. Nevertheless, the phrase sure does seem to fit the unconscious processes being described. The success of computers also establishes, I think conclusively, that characteristics once thought to be solely the domain of conscious entities—the machinations of "thinking" and the display of "intelligence"—do not require consciousness at all. Machines can *think*, and they can display *intelligence*. We might find it difficult to accept that at first because those words are loaded with preconceived notions of implied consciousness. We might believe that granting such characteristics to a machine would also, by implication, be granting machines the extra characteristic of consciousness. But that's not so. A computer doesn't possess consciousness. But machines can still think and display intelligence.

Not convinced? Let's consider human thinking for a second. Here's Jayne's again:

[T]here are several stages of creative thought: first, a stage of preparation in which the problem is consciously worked over; then a
period of incubation without any conscious concentration upon the
problem; and then the illumination which is later justified by
logic...The period of preparation is essentially the setting up of a
complex structure together with the conscious attention to the
materials on which the structure is to work. But then the actual
process of reasoning, the dark leap into huge discovery,..., has no
representation in consciousness, Indeed, it is sometimes almost as if
the problem had to be forgotten to be solved.

I think we can all relate to this sort of experience; banging our heads, banging our heads, we get no results. Then we kind of put the problem away for a
spell, take a break, and without directly thinking about our problem, like
magic we finally either solve the problem or understand something we previously couldn't. Like a brain-fart gone *good*. This raises the frustratingly paradoxical possibility that our own thoughts are ultimately processes beyond our
control; birds upon birds flying in an unconscious aviary, and we only conscious of those most dwelled upon.

There are many machinations going on in our heads that we are unconscious
of. Consciousness seemingly pervades everything that we do and we are seemingly conscious at all times. But this is really an illusion. An illusion brought on by
the humorously deceptive truth that we can only be conscious of things that we
are conscious of. If we do sort of "space out" or lapse into a state of *un*conscious-
experience, we wouldn't be conscious of having done so, so we would be unable to
report on it. But I think things like that occur. And probably a lot more frequently
than we could ever guess. Judging by the concert pianist, an athlete that enters
"the zone," or the thinker taking a break—paradoxically, such unconscious-expe-
riences might be some of the most enviable states one can achieve. Notice, however, that there's no free lunch. A conscious time of extreme practice and work is
needed before you can get the desired results.

As mentioned earlier, my intuition is that there is a fundamental characteristic of life-forms: that characteristic being unconscious-experience.
Unfortunately, I don't know of a way that this can be proved.

The phenomenon called *blindsight* is often brought up among philosophy-
of-mind types, and some even believe it provides evidence for what zombiness
of unconscious experience might be like. Blindsight is a particular affliction
that produces an effect of zombie-like unconsciousness in an otherwise normal,

conscious person. It happens when the visual pathways in the brain have been severed. A spot in the visual field lacks content, implying a *scotoma*, a blindness in that area of vision. However, those possessing blindsight display a most peculiar talent. Despite having no conscious visual experience in that area, and stating as much to be the case, the person evidently makes up for this deficit through different information channels. These different information channels derive, evidently, from the human eye. However, the procedure is *automatic*, unconscious. While not paranormal, the net effect is that the person sees without having the *awareness* of seeing—guessing shapes, the direction of motion, and the presence or absence of light at a rate much better than chance. (Dennett, 1991) All the same, the information *is* being transmitted, and the person—at some stage in the procedure—*becomes aware* of that transmission (especially with fast-moving motion), so that he or she can communicate their near-perfect predictions. Otherwise, the guesses simply would not be consistently above chance. Is blindsight really an example of what zombiness might be like as it is sometimes claimed? Certainly, a complication is introduced by posing a sub-set of zombiness inside of an otherwise conscious framework. I can be unconscious of ongoing processes of ear-wax build up, but still be all-too-aware of the predictable results. Having awareness in the equation makes it very difficult to prove anything. Obviously, my leanings happen to favor the meaningfulness of the term "unconscious experience," but even with the suggestiveness of blindsight I really don't believe anything has been conclusively proven.

However this may be, I yet believe that all the higher-order systems found in humans are patched-together add-ons to a more underlying basic program. Further, I think we can occasionally detect this lower-level program in ourselves, as in the previous examples.

Want a provocative thought? What if I suggested that perception might be an unconscious function? That perception, the ability to perceive, by itself does not mean you're conscious?

In a way, doesn't this make perfect sense?

How can we really expect that all animals having the ability of sight are conscious?

These are rhetorical questions, intended to provoke. But such questions do give one pause for thought. Consciousness could well be a higher-level function to processes that otherwise are unconscious. There's something mind-expanding about that thought. Something crazy, yet compelling. Could all our sense perceptions, in and of themselves, be unconscious functions? Can it really be possible to be a thing that experiences—with the functions of sight, smells, and touch (or in an amoeba's case functions far more basic)—and yet be a thing that is unconscious?

The nonintuitive answer, I believe, is *yes*.

The idea of unconscious-experience might be hard to accept, let alone understand. But I think it's definitely worth consideration. Note that the number zero took a very long time to crystallize in the history of thought. The number zero is an intrinsic paradox, a paradox that we forget about due to familiarity. Zero is a *number* assigned to *nothing*. In much the same way, I think the idea of unconscious-experience is a paradox, but no less true (possibly) because of it.

I think there's a good chance that unconscious-experience is found in all life, and that life is ultimately A Variation on a Theme—a Theme that itself was an unconscious-experiencer.

BYTE TEN:

MYSTICAL
EXPERIENCES

http://www.philscanlan.net/

Mystical Experiences

For the great philosopher David Hume [so great in fact that it makes one wonder how he *could* have been so prophetic in almost all of his thinking and yet be a philosopher—is it a probability thing?—thousands of philosophers through history all speculating wildly, someone's bound to be "correct"?!], the self is not an entity for it is not an object of perception since there is no specific impression corresponding to "I." [He somewhat similarly denies causality as usually considered on the grounds that there are no logical connections between events.] He famously wrote:

> For my part, when I enter most intimately into what I call myself, I always tumble on some particular perception or other, of heat or cold, light or shade, love or hatred, pain or pleasure. I never catch myself at any time without a perception, and never can observe anything but the perception. (*Treatise*, Book I, Pat iv, Sect. 6)

Ironically, this view coming from an empiricist is very similar to conclusions drawn by idealist eastern philosophies. The "self" is illusory. It's a bundle of make-believe that really isn't there after all. The entire goal of most eastern philosophies is to extinguish perceptions altogether in meditation to achieve a nirvana state. Interestingly, there might be a connection with computational theory in this. If one really can reach a state of "no perceptions"—then what kind of brain-state does that imply? A very curious one!

Hindu Mysticism (*The Upanishads*)

From the *Chandoga Upanishad:*

> "As by knowing one lump of clay,…, we come to know all things made out of clay: that they differ only in name and form, while the stuff of which all are made is clay; as by knowing one gold nugget,…, we come to know all things made out of gold: that they differ only in name and form, while the stuff of which all are made is gold; as by knowing one tool of iron,…, we come to know all things made out

of iron: that they differ only in name and form, while the stuff of which all are made is iron—so through that spiritual wisdom,…, we come to know that all of life is one.…

In the beginning was only Being, one without a second. Out of himself he brought forth the cosmos and entered into everything in it. There is nothing that does not come from him. Of everything he is the inmost Self. He is the truth; he is the Self supreme. You are that.…

As the rivers flowing east and west merge in the sea and become one with it, forgetting they were ever separate rivers, so do all creatures lose their separateness when they merge at last into pure Being. There is nothing that does not come from him. Of everything he is the inmost Self. He is the truth; he is the Self supreme. You are that."

Plotinus' Mysticism

From The Writings of Plotinus:

> …[T]he time will come when it will enjoy the vision without interruption, no longer troubled with the hindrances of the body. The part of the Soul which is troubled is not the part which sees, but the other part, when the part which sees is idle, though it ceases not from that knowledge which comes of demonstrations, conjectures, and the dialectic. But in the vision that which sees is not reason, but something greater than and prior to reason, something presupposed by reason, as is the object of vision. He who then sees himself, when he sees will see himself as a simple being, will be united to himself as such, will feel himself become such. We ought not even to say that he will *see*, but he will *be* that which he sees, if indeed it is possible any longer to distinguish seer and seen, and not boldly to affirm that the two are one. In this state the seer does not see or distinguish or imagine two things; he becomes another, he ceases to be himself and to belong to himself. He belongs to Him and is one with Him, like concentric circles; they are one when they coincide, and two only when they are separated. It is only in this sense that the Soul is other [than God]. Therefore this vision is hard to describe. For how can one

describe, as other than oneself, that which, when one saw it, seemed to be one with oneself?...

Christian Mysticism

From *Sermon 6:*

> Nothing hinders the soul's knowledge of God as much as time and space, for time and space are fragments, whereas God is one! And therefore, if the soul is to know God, it must know him above time and outside of space; for God is neither this nor that, as are these manifold things. God is One!

From *Sermon 22:*

> ...[W]e are not wholly blessed, even though we are looking at divine truth; for while we are still looking at it, we are not in it. As long as a man has an object under consideration, he is not one with it. Where there is nothing but One, nothing but One is to be seen. Therefore, no man can see God except he be blind, nor know him except through ignorance, nor understand him except through folly.

Taoist Mysticism

From the *Tao-Te King:*

> The Tao that can be expressed is not the eternal Tao; the name that can be defined is not the unchanging name. Non-existence is called the antecedent of heaven and earth; existence is the mother of all things. From eternal non-existence, therefore, we serenely observe the mysterious beginning of the universe; from eternal existence we clearly see the apparent distinctions. These two are the same in source and become different when manifested. This sameness is called profundity. Infinite profundity is the gate whence comes the beginning of all parts of the universe.

Buddhist Mysticism

From The *Hinayana Selections:*

> There is,…, that plane where there is neither extension nor…motion nor the plane of infinite ether…nor that of neither-perception-nor-non-perception, neither this world nor another, neither the Moon nor the sun. Here,…, I say that there is no coming or going or remaining or decreasing or uprising, for this is itself without support, without continuance, without mental object—this is itself the end of suffering.

> There is,…, an unborn, not become, not made, uncompounded, and were it not,…, for this unborn, not become, not made, uncompounded, no escape could be shown here for what is born, has become, is made, is compounded. But because there is,…, an unborn, not become, not made, uncompounded, therefore an escape can be shown for what is born, has become, is made, is compounded.

The most obvious explanations for all these mystical experiences is that they are **either** indicative of a meta-physical x—in which case these experiences are "true" glimpses into a super-reality beyond our normal waking senses, **or** products of hallucination—in which case these experiences are products of aberrant brain states. While a meta-physical x is fairly self-explanatory and not very interesting for our present purposes (especially since it's definitionally meaningless to "see" something that cannot be seen), the hallucination-hypothesis provides a plausible explanation that doesn't appeal to the inexplicable or the illogical. In point of fact, I consider it self-evident that mystical experiences are experiences that take place in the mind—they are, for lack of a better term, "hallucinations." All the same, I find it infuriating when certain supposed *intellectuals* attempt to "explain" mystical experiences as hallucinations without even bothering to adequately define what is meant by hallucinations.

The answer seems to be that our perceptual system cannot always be sure what is "real" and what isn't. Noisy and unreliable input can threaten the input model—along with perhaps a failure of inhibition—making the normally less stable models seem stronger and more real than otherwise warranted. At such a point, our perceptual system might well be forced into accepting an inferior model of reality as real, only to be replaced when conditions for a better model prevail. Such conditions of unreliability are precisely those needed to induce strange experiences. Inputs of stress, fear, epilepsy, migraine headaches, sensory deprivation, falling asleep, dreaming, among many others, all could conceivably play a factor in near-death experiences. These very conditions make it exceedingly difficult for our perceptual system to make the correct determination of "real."

A curious non-starter arises whenever we start questioning *why* our brains might have the function of a "God-Experience." What if, as might well be the case, we can activate brain-tissue *here* and produce subjective "God-experiences" *every* time? What does that prove? Has anything really been *explained*, or is there really no explanation possible, just a bunch of interesting stuff that happens?

Following are some examples of hallucinations; some bordering on the mystical, others swimming in it—pre-categorized for your reading pleasure.

Easy

When starting this book, I wrote intensely for a month. In that time, while resting in bed before sleep, I would occasionally "see" before me line after line of "pre-made" sentences that existed as if all by themselves. My guess is that the phenomenon of "after-images"—an image that remains/endures even after the external stimulus is withdrawn (i.e., "seeing" a blue spot on a white paper after staring at a yellow dot for a long enough time)—accounts for such things. This is not unlike when playing a video game like Tetris long enough, after-images of the game can be "seen" while later reading a book, or doing some other activity. In my view, this type of experience has an iron-clad physiological basis and is well-accounted for without having to appeal to "mysticism."

Consider another example from Carl Sagan:

> Sometimes I dream that I'm talking to my parents, and suddenly—still immersed in the dreamwork—I'm seized by the overpowering realization that they didn't really die, that it's all been some kind of horrible mistake. Why, here they are, alive and well, my father making wry jokes, my mother earnestly advising me to wear a muffler because the weather is chilly. When I wake up, I go through an abbreviated process of mourning all over again. Plainly, there's something within me that's ready to believe in life and death. And it's not the least bit interested in whether there's any sober evidence for it.

Sagan here lets us in on his very odd secret. I say "secret" because these sorts of mystical dreams are not something generally talked about. The reason being, perhaps, because there is not much to say about them. Sagan had a dream about his dead parents. What is there really more to say—in polite conversation or otherwise? All the same, I've had similar dreams—recurring—about a dead brother that I pleasantly dream-discover to be alive. I had thought he was dead, but I had been mistaken. Sometimes, during the dream I remember having had the same realization before (in other dreams) and I wonder "why did I ever think he was dead in the first place?"

Another interesting example of dream-mysticism is that of the following:

> A common,…, psychological syndrome rather like alien abduction is called sleep paralysis…It happens in that twilight between being fully awake and fully asleep. For a few minutes, maybe longer, you're immobile and acutely anxious. You feel a weight on your chest as if some being is sitting or lying there. Your heartbeat is quick, your breathing labored. You may experience auditory or visual hallucinations—of people, demons, ghosts, animals, or birds. In the right setting, the experience can have "the full force and impact of reality," according to Robert Baker, a psychologist at the University of Kentucky…Baker argues that these common sleep disturbances are behind many if not most of the alien abduction accounts…

> We know from early work of the Canadian neurophysiologist Wilder Penfield that electrical stimulation of certain regions of the brain elicits full-blown hallucinations. People with temporal lobe epilepsy—involving a cascade of naturally generated electrical impulses in the part of the brain beneath the forehead—experience a range of hallucinations almost indistinguishable from reality: including the presence of one or more strange beings, anxiety, floating through the air, sexual experiences, and a sense of missing time. There is also what feels like profound insight into the deepest questions and a need to spread the word. A continuum of spontaneous temporal lobe stimulation seems to stretch from people with serious epilepsy to the most average among us…So such hallucinations, generated spontaneously, or with chemical or experiential assists, may play a role—perhaps a central role—in the UFO accounts.

I've had such an experience of sleep paralysis at least once. It occurred after having awoken and then falling back to sleep. Perhaps I had slept too long, I don't know, and I'm not so sure it really matters. Regardless of the reason, I found that *I could not wake up*. I lay motionless as if fastened down—unable to move—in a sort of quasi-dreamstate. I "saw" that red worms were falling on me and I was unable to get myself up and away. I remember this vividly, although it occurred quite a few years ago. That some people may choose to interpret such quirky experiences as UFO abductions I find entirely plausible. By the way, I have chosen to give first-person accounts in the examples above for a very specific reason. Namely, I believe these types of experiences are ubiquitous—infrequently experienced by one and all, destined, for the most point, to be forgotten.

All the same, these count as "easy" examples of mysticism. If one delights in ridiculing experiences such as those cited above, that's fine, however, I do not find that to be much of an accomplishment. After all, these examples are of after-images and dreams. How sporting is that?

Middling

It is a well-known curious fact that many important ideas and solutions to problems did not originate in the context of logical reasoning, but in various unusual states of mind—in dreams, while falling asleep or awakening, at times of extreme physical and mental fatigue, or during an illness with high fever. There are many famous examples of this. The chemist Friedrich August von Kekulé arrived at the final solution of the chemical formula of benzene in a dream in which he saw the benzene ring in the form of a snake biting its tail. Nikola Tesla constructed the electric generator, an invention that revolutionized industry, after the complete design of it appeared to him in great detail in a vision. The design for the experiment leading to the Nobel prize-winning discovery of the chemical transmission of nerve impulses occurred to the physiologist Otto Loewi while he was asleep. Albert Einstein discovered the basic principles of his special theory of relativity in an unusual state of mind; according to his description, most of the insights came to him in the form of kinaesthetic sensations.

We could mention many instances of a similar kind where a creative individual struggled unsuccessfully for a long time with a difficult problem using logic and reason, with the actual solution emerging unexpectedly from the unconscious in moments when his or her rationality was suspended.

Consider some other less obvious examples of mystical insight:

The [Mendelbrot] set is...a geometrical form known as a "fractal," which is closely related to the theory of chaos...The set is generated by successive applications of the rule (or mapping) $z \rightarrow z^2 + c$, where z is a complex number and c is a certain fixed complex number. The rule simply means: pick a complex number z and replace it with $z^2 + c$, then take this number to be z and make the same replacement, and so on, again and again. The successive complex numbers can be plotted on a sheet of paper (or a computer screen) as the rule is applied, each number represented as a dot. What is found is that for some choices of c the dot soon leaves the screen. For other choices, however, the dot wanders about forever within the bounded region. Now, each choice of c itself corresponds to a dot on the screen. The collection of all such c-dots forms the Mandelbrot set...A distinctive feature of the Mandelbrot set is that any portion of it may be magnified again and again without limit, and each new layer of resolution brings forth new riches and delights.

Penrose remarks that, when Mandelbrot embarked on his study of the set, he had no real prior conception of the fantastic elaboration inherent in it:

The complete details of the complication of the structure of Mandelbrot's set cannot really be fully comprehended by any one of us, nor can it be fully revealed by any computer. It would seem that this structure is not just part of our minds, but it has a reality of its own...The computer is being used in essentially the same way that the experimental physicist uses a piece of experimental apparatus to explore the structure of the physical world. The Mandelbrot set is not an invention of the human mind: it was a discovery. Like Mount Everest, the Mandelbrot set is just there!

Platonism, according to physicist Roger Penrose in his book *The Emperor's New Mind*, suggests that mathematical objects and rules exist independently from us, transcending our physical reality (see, I told you I'd be returning to this!). According to this view, mathematicians are uncovering truths that are already "out there." Penrose even suggests that some of these things—like the Mendelbrot set—can be toured as if they were physical things. Whether your vehicle is a computer program or your own mind, the mathematical set being toured is one and the same thing. Penrose wants to show us that the set is an object—a pattern that objectively exists. There is an intuitiveness about this view, although the strength of the pull depends largely upon one's initial assumptions. Consider another example:

> The French mathematician Jacques Hadamard made a study of this [breaking through] phenomenon, and cites the case of Carl Gauss, who had for years been wrestling with a problem about whole numbers: "Like a sudden flash of lightning, the riddle happened to be solved. I myself cannot say what was the conducting thread which connected what I previously knew with what made my success possible." Hadamard also gives the famous case of Henri Poincaré set, who had likewise spent a lot of time fruitlessly tackling a problem concerning certain mathematical functions. One day Poincaré set out on a geological excursion, and went to board the bus. "At the moment when I put my foot on the step, the idea came to me, without anything in my former thoughts seeming to have paved the way for it," he reported. So certain was he that the problem was solved that he put it to the back of his mind and continued his conversation. When he returned from the trip he was able to prove the result readily, at his leisure.

Examples like these imply that the "answers" are out there, floating around somewhere and can be discovered suddenly, as if sent by an angel. Poets, writers, and other creative sorts often speak of experiencing such sudden flashes of inspiration. Again, the *pull* such examples may have depends largely upon one's initial assumptions. I happen to find the pull of these considerations to be *very* strong indeed. Considered by themselves, however, the evidence remains ambiguous. Brain-states or Platonic-states? Who knows! I sure don't. And so long as the evidence remains ambiguous, I think the assumption must go with *brain-states*. But it's still mighty unclear whether brain-states are sufficient to account for all the anomalies. Occasionally anomalies have a way of building upon themselves so as to culminate in a breaking point. And then one contextual system collapses in favor of another. I don't think we are quite there yet, but be ever aware!

A Real Pickle of a Pickle

Whether the Fundamental Reality is described as One (Plotinus), God (Christian mystics), Self-God (Hindu mystics), Nothingness (Buddha), or

Whatever Else (Nature mystics and so on), there's a *possibility* that these apparent differences are cosmetic and belie an underlying sameness, but others notice only the significant and very real differences. Some believe that the Fundamental Reality is so complex, mysterious, and ungraspable that it can only be talked about and referred to in contradictory (paradoxical?) terms. Any which way, mystical experiences are inherently ambiguous. At least to some extent, they must be products of brain-states. Any mystical or near-death experience that anybody has ever had has always been a living person having brain-states. Whatever the deep, meaningful insight the mystical or near-death experience provides the individual, it's another question entirely as to whether or not that individual will be capable of "seeing" any of that revelation upon death.

The reason I bring this up? I've had such an experience myself: a "near-death experience." And boy was it contradictory. Here we go then. First, I'm going to present the experience as remembered, and then I'll offer some analysis.

The Experience

While still in college, I experimented with a certain chemical which shall remain nameless. As it should happen, I soon developed a most throbbing point-like pain in my head. The pain was awesome—far from being merely a headache or a bout of migraines. There was nothing but this throbbing pain in my head, and when I tried to think, my thoughts were child-like. My thinking was slow, plodding, and I was not capable of making connections (and no that's not typical for me, regardless of the sprawling incoherence you see before you). This is when my near-death experience began and my physical body (unbeknownst to me) went into convulsions—apparently not unlike an epileptic seizure.

First, there was the proverbial tunnel. This tunnel, through which I seemed to "travel" in a forward motion, was composed of my past experiences. These past experiences ended soon enough, but I kept "traveling" in a forward motion. There was no "light" at the end of this tunnel, despite my having read previously that there should have been. [Of course, some could suggest here that they could have predicted this seeing as though I wasn't lying under the bright light of an operating table as is typical for those undergoing such a near-death experience.] My senses seemed completely blocked off from the outside world and I developed the belief that I was coming to an answer. The answer to the question that most vexed me—"how is there anything at all?"

As I "traveled" forward, things were becoming more intense, more fundamental. It was as if things were becoming more "real"—indeed, it seemed as though actual reality was about to reveal itself. Understand that I regarded this experience at the time as being of profound importance.

Eventually, I reached the pinnacle—the end of the tunnel. This "end" seemed to be a puzzle—an incomplete puzzle. More succinctly, it was a contradiction. A contradiction that was nevertheless true—thus making it a paradox. The nature of this paradox was that "existence" existed purely by default. There was a sort of Yin-Yang, an eternal war, between existence and nonexistence. Which of the two should be the state of things? Neither, both, either? It was undecidable. For who decided? How *could* it be decided? Yet the state of things *must* be either existing or nonexisting. This seemed fundamental.

Then I noticed a very strange thing. These things—existence and nonexistence—didn't really exist. They couldn't—for it wasn't decided whether things existed or not. Yet this fundamental potentiality was provoking the "thought" that there must be either existence or nonexistence. And I realized that *this very thought must exist* to "think" these potentialities. In this case, I view "think" as simply the place where these potentialities—these abstractions—took place (meaning that it's not clear that this "think" had a personality, as it can be viewed as a strictly computational process). Any which way, existence had been decided by default. I recall having mixed feelings about this new insight. I considered it profound. However, I was also sad that that's all it boiled down to— that there was nothing deeper, more meaningful. Yet, I realized at the same time how beautiful it was—how that's the way it *had* to be. It was *impossible* for things to have been otherwise. *Impossible* for there to have been nonexistence—not *a priori* impossible, but impossible all the same.

That's the meat of my experience. Despite my "seizure," I regained my consciousness *fully energized*. I had a new dedication and respect for life that I had quite frankly lacked previously, and which continues to this day. Simply put, this experience *changed my life*.

So what can be made of all this?

As I hope you can appreciate, this question has perplexed me for years. Recall that these types of experiences, by definition, have a most profound impact upon the subject. I couldn't help but view this experience as deeply meaningful, and I myself as somehow "special" and "unique" for having experienced it. These things should go without saying. Many years have now passed since that day, and I have had much time to consider and reconsider the nature of the experience. Following is a brief encapsulation of what I have to say about it.

Upshot

Now first of all, why am I even discussing this? Obviously, I'm leaving myself wide open for attack. Any critic of my overall agenda can condemn it by simply pointing to its "mystic" origins. I understand this. There are people who could care less that it's faulty reasoning to deny the argument due to its inspiration; the benzine ring is the benzine ring regardless that it derived from a dream. The argument and the inspiration for that argument are two different things. The valid way to refute The Script would be by refuting The Script directly—not by condemning the nature of my inspiration for The Script.

I include it for the sake of pure, naked honesty. This is how it happened. This is the original source of my "inspiration." The experience has resulted in this book. I thirst to figure this stuff out—existence/nonexistence, hallucinations, the nature of such a profoundly meaningful "near-death experience." *That's* the inspiration. The dilemma is trying to figure out the nature of brain-states, the physical stuff of which we're composed, such that it can sufficiently explain such deep experiences. It is not enough to say "your experience was merely an hallucination and an hallucination is merely an aberrant brain-state." Such non-answers do not help us unveil the mask of reality. Why is reality the way it is? Why do we dream? Why do we even think at all? However…

Like a hot potato I hereby drop this near-death experience from further discussion. Why? Because I have no place to go with it. Rationally, I am forced to dismiss the experience as hallucinatory and dream-like, a mammoth brain-fart I once had, even though I recall it as much, much more. This *forced to* is caused by my inability to reproduce that experience or in any way confirm its central claim in relation to that past experience. What I *can do*, however, is formulate an argument (The Script) that originated from it. This argument stands on its own merits, regardless of whatever the true nature of the inspiration may be.

Conclusion: Perhaps there are certain algorithmic patterns in the brain that are attainable: algorithmic patterns that map to a more fundamental/basic/low-level reality. And perhaps some of the paradoxical accounts given from mystical experiences make more sense in this light.

Mysterians

Human consciousness might be a fluky add-on to a far more basic and widespread program of unconscious experience. No matter how many times a new universe is born, that new universe will ultimately produce unconscious experience—the Variations are many, but the Theme is one. As far as predictions go, however, such a view lacks practicality. In fact, the very contention that some form of consciousness is fundamental is usually associated with the mysterians.

The mysterian position views the mind-body problem to be unsolvable. Why? Because it is asserted that we are cognitively limited and thus incapable of answering such a question. To me, this assertion seems to be a can of worms. Does that mean we can never even *come close* to the answer? Does that mean we can never even be *reasonably certain* about any given answer's correctness? And if not, WHY NOT? How can anyone possibly really know that??? (It's just an assumption that's been made, and I think an assumption leading nowhere.)

The mysterian position is difficult to accept. Lurking beneath their heady talk of cognitive limitations (and note that I am a proponent of limitations as well, it's just that I believe that it's outright impossible for us to know what those limitations actually tell us) is a demand that consciousness be made knowable *Absolutely Positively*. So sorry, but that's not the world we live in.

The modern world has opened avenues before us like never before. We have computers that are becoming more and more intelligent, capable even of beating chess-master's at their own game. While machines as yet lack consciousness, it is clear that at least some of the underlying processes that work for humans also work for machines—for we only need to look at the very success of computers. Always remember that we ourselves are products of this world, and that the world is not our product. We exist as conscious beings, conscious machines. Our consciousness resides at the top-most level of a largely mechanical system that functions in spite of ourselves. We don't consciously "tell" our brain to keep breathing, keep our hearts beating, and so on. Those things happen mechanically, on a level beneath our consciousness.

So we know that systems such as ourselves are possible, by the patch-worked hand of nature's Blind Programmer. Machines, of course, are made by humans, but both humans and machines exist in nature and their respective successes are limited to what the world allows. That computer processes work so successfully should give us pause for thought. But viewing the brain as a formal algorithm is simply not the correct way of looking at things, and presents a straw-man if there ever was one.

The primary difficulty comes by way of the high level of *messiness* involved. Machines are just not messy enough. They lack emotion, and the chemical balances and imbalances that go along with that. They have "intelligence," but not creative intelligence—computers are capable of doing the mechanical process of collecting more and more data to support an existing hard-wired opinion/value/agenda, yet never having the ability of transcending that initial position with a new, greater understanding. Machines are already intelligent, right now, today. However, because modern-day intelligent machines never evolved as part of the environment, they have no way of interacting with that environment. The machines are not cognizant because they lack emotion (emotion being broadly defined as the give-and-take, stimulus/response process of interacting with the environment); hence they can never be capable of transcending their programmed input until they can emote and interact with the environment. So, perhaps the human brain does not work like a single computer, but rather a super-computer—a collection of computers working in parallel tandem. Perhaps also our somewhat illusory idea of "self" is cumulatively hardwired into our synapses as we travel along in life from experience to experience, developing our "self" in a 20 Questions kind of way as we go. And, perhaps, even this sense of self can be machine-duplicated. Yes, there's a lot at play. And none of these thoughts are particularly new.

A Variation on a Theme implies the following predictions: unconscious experience is both computational and reproducible—*it wants to happen.* However, there may exist a severe limitation as to just *how reproducible* unconscious experience really is, especially concerning our form of awareness. For example, turning a dead machine into a mind may prove less analogous to recreating a fire-spark and more analogous to turning lead into gold. While gold is composed of certain chemicals and must have arisen in nature due to some determinate process, it doesn't therefore follow that we can actually convert lead into gold. Similarly, just because a mind is composed of certain computations and must have arisen in nature due to some determinate process, it doesn't therefore follow that we can actually convert a dead machine into mind. In short, it might be a trick and a half to reproduce an accident of such epic proportions.

That's the problem with analogies. You can never quite tell which one is accurate until *after* an appropriate empirical investigation. After all, perhaps nanobots can one day be designed to manipulate the *very atoms* inside lead, and by so doing *convert lead into gold*. While this idea may seem fanciful now, as Arthur C. Clarke once wisely put it, "Any sufficiently advanced technology is

indistinguishable from magic." Even if *mind-making* seems sort of like *gold-making*, both possibilities remain open-ended.

Some might still be confused as to what, if anything, has really been said about consciousness, let alone unconscious-experience, as to what it's like and how it works. Well, consider the following excerpt from philosopher David Chalmers" *The Conscious Mind* :

> What is it that allows such diverse phenomena as reproduction, learning, and heat to be reductively explained? In all these cases, the nature of the concepts required to characterize the phenomena is crucial. If someone objected to a cellular explanation of reproduction, "this explains how a cellular process can lead to the production of a complex physical entity that is similar to the original entity, but it doesn't explain *reproduction*," we would have little patience—for that is all that "reproduction" *means*. (Chalmers, 1996)

While the wording here might seem a tad obscure, the thought behind the wording is rather simple. A problematical *ghost* can be made out of a process like reproduction, such that it can be staunchly held that no valid account can be given for it. However, after a time we find that we have to *give up the ghost*. After a time, we are forced to admit to ourselves that the explanation for reproduction (or anything else for that matter) will never be quite as *meaningful* as we might once have hoped. In a similar manner, I think that our "consciousness" (our peculiar add-on to a deeper level unconscious-experience) has no *meaning* outside of the default computation encapsulated by the Theme, as Varied by our universe. We're conscious because our universe is a sort of computation that *demands* there to be unconscious-experience, while *allowing for* higher-order add-ons. Unconscious-experience wants to happen, and it can happen again and again and again (even in ways that might now be viewed as "artificial").

Most likely the re-creation of *aliveness* and *unconscious-experience* will only be achieved when the existing, default, process of *natural selection* is appropriately utilized. After all, the game is not merely to create complex wirings and involved algorithms. A dead human's brain is just as complexly structured as a living human's brain, yet there's an obvious difference in ability between the two. Aliveness and experience, therefore, can not possibly be *only* a product of complexity. They might actually *require* the process of natural selection.

Help for us in re-creating the process of natural selection might be found in the nanotechnologies. Microscopic robots made out of proteins could one day be designed to perform that very simple task called *replication* (hopefully this would be done in a "sped up," controlled environment—and let's make sure it's *controlled* less the replicating nanobots become a humanity-destroying virus!). Replication is all it would need to do—not that it's presently even close to happening. Nanomachines the width of a human hair have already been made, they just don't necessarily work very well yet. Regardless, so long as the robot was flexible enough, using for instance an imperfect TIT-FOR-TAT strategy (mimicking the imperfection of genetic variation), it would seem that the process of evolution would very probably take over from there and complete the process very quickly and automatically (naturally).

Narrative's End

I want to give you a full sense of the problem of consciousness as I see it. As has been reiterated time and again in this book, the human mind needs to use analogies for the comprehension of abstract matters. When it comes to conscious experience itself, however, there is not and cannot be anything available to us that it is like (aside from the phenomenon itself). Frustratingly, I don't believe it possible to understand consciousness in the same manner that we can understand other things; because it's impossible to make a model of it. *Impossible.* Saying it's "like a computer" is not a model in this sense. The process underlying experience might very well be like a computer, or at least a very messy one, however saying this does not provide a model of experience proper. Hard-core functionalists want the metaphor of "like a computer" to collapse the distinction between *processes* and *experiences* by claiming they are one and the same thing. Note that even if we *acknowledge* this collapsing of a formidable dichotomy and agree that the dichotomy between body and mind is ultimately a false dichotomy (as I believe it to be), *our individual unique experience* would still be unexplained. Processes can only explain *experience in the abstract*. The *particular* urgency of our experience is not captured.

Is not awareness an inherent *essence* or *quality* that we possess? Is not awareness that which identifies our inner most being? How can *that* be studied scientifically? Isn't human awareness the foundational necessity upon which the entire construct of science depends? Is there really a way to "step outside" of science (which inherently depends upon our human awareness) to "objectively" study human awareness? Doesn't that just smack of attempting to create a meta-science, which would in turn necessitate a meta-meta-science, and so on and so forth, infinitely and beyond?

Well, we can't step outside of ourselves, so we're left clueless and frustrated. Consider the dualist option, the functionalist option, and the mysterian option. Each option represents a distinct interpretive branch in the study of consciousness that can be further subdivided into a full spectrum of available opinions. At the extremes you have "consciousness is illusory" and "consciousness is fundamental." In philosopher David Chalmers' *The Conscious Mind* he suggests that some *outside condition* must be necessary to fully explain *consciousness*. For Chalmers, this *outside condition* takes the form of some *brand-new* fundamental law that accounts for consciousness. Clearly, I'm not in particular disagreement with what Chalmers is suggesting since if looked at abstractly enough my Variation on a Theme could be viewed as "the greater reason/law" behind consciousness that Chalmers apparently wants. But I can't fully accept that as I find such answers unsatisfying. The generic supposition that "everything is but A Variation on a Theme" is as stultifyingly weak as any other blanket description of the world, whether that be materialism, subjectivism or anything else. Such grand conjectures should be likened to frameworks, with the caveat that a frame doesn't *explain* the picture it surrounds, it just makes it presentable (which is important in its own right). So too is it with A Variation on a Theme. A frame can't explain. And the frustration that comes from contemplation of consciousness derives from trying to explain it with all its particularities. Even if we grant the insight that the Theme from which our universe is but a Variation was itself "unconscious," we don't know for sure what such an "unconsciousness" is *like*, let alone the long, strange trip that was taken to get to *our* kind of consciousness. That's the problem with generalities, you lose the particularities. And in a way, I think that's the problem with the human condition, we're stuck in a conflict, a paradox, an uncertainty principle, an undecidability theorem. We can cast a net around "everything," but then all the particulars fall through, or we can grab at the particulars but then the conception of "everything" disappears. That's paradox. That's the limits of our human conception.

Perhaps it's time I introduce you to my religion. And I mean it; *my religion*. My belief system. I believe that given our ridiculous situation in attempting to self-consciously comment upon our own self-consciousness, we are forced to adhere to rough and fundamentally arbitrary rules of thumb. This is true for any early stage of investigation for any given phenomenon, scientific or otherwise. We are forced to start with working definitions—arbitrary axioms—

rather than complete theories. In science, such "working thumbs" are called hypotheses. In life, it's called the *process of learning*. We don't understand everything there is to know about a bicycle all in one gulp. It's a cumulative process. We ride it and fall down a few times. And then we grow more familiar with its nuances and become more and more experienced to its temperamental ways. And, finally, joyously, we tame the Beast. We own the bicycle. But at no point did we gain FULL enlightenment of "bicycleness." There's no such thing. Likewise, I believe "consciousness" is a concept that will never admit to FULL enlightenment. It's fundamentally arbitrary and meaningless. Our brains possess multitudes of mini-computers that just happened to produce the phenomenon we experience as experience. That "just happened to" part is the point that is most frustrating. Identifying experience with brain processes, as must be done, doesn't provide any great insight into the "just happened to" that produces the experienced phenomenon itself. Of course, denying the link to the brain just deepens the mystery further, so that's really not even an option. And so we're left with arbitrariness. It just works that way. Much like gravity just works that way, or electricity, or photosynthesis. There's nothing deeper. That arbitrariness equates to meaninglessness. There's no real meaning. Yet, as soon as we say that it's meaningless, we're caught in idle speculation as whatever "meaning" there may be is contained within our experience in the first place. So, paradoxically, there has to be meaning because our very experience is meaningful, while at the same time being meaningless.

This is why I believe that the Script is itself an unconscious-experiencer. Because I believe the same principle works in that context as well as our context. Experience might arise simply because that's how things work. You can't have a necessarily existing conflict without there being an experience of that conflict. And since that conflict is caught in a paradox such that the "Law of non-Contradiction" absurdly, ridiculously, meaninglessly *both* applies and does not apply at one and the same time, it is forced to metaphorically explode. So we have a Script that is the product of utter absurdity, utter ridiculousness, utter meaninglessness. But that very same Script is also necessarily existing. It had to be that way, it was *forced* to be that way—which means that it's as meaningful as meaningful can get. Yet it's meaning*less*. That's what I like about the Script. I think it captures Truth, because it shows how all of reality can be both meaningless and meaningful at one and the same time (and I think that is the only supposition that has a chance at being correct).

Switching back to human experience, in philosopher Daniel Dennett's *Consciousness Explained*, he tells a story about "Multiple Drafts"—the general idea of which I believe to be true—suggesting that consciousness itself is illusory. I'm attracted to this position because it is both meaningless and meaningful at one and the same time. After all, if I wanted to "know" that everything was *maya* (illusory), couldn't I have just studied the Eastern Religions? In fact, let's press the point a little further. Let's assume that profoundly speaking, *everything* we take for granted is basically illusory and mistaken. Undoubtedly, this is correct to some degree. I think our understanding of things is at such a low-grade level that our wrongness about certain things has probably compounded upon itself over the years, creating an insurmountable amount of confusion: a plight easily seen with the clumsy distinction that we try to make between *consciousness* and *unconscious-experience*. But then you start asking yourself, "hey, *according to what* exactly is all of our experiences illusory?" And then we see how arbitrary all this really is. Our human experience (especially our human *intellectual* experience) demands an *according to*; we cannot get outside of it. Hence, whenever someone makes a claim that the very reality of *"according to"* is itself illusory, a metaphysical claim is being made *according to* so-and-so that amounts to unsupportable metaphysics. We can't get outside of that *according to*. We do not have access to an objective Book of Truth that somehow circumvents this intrinsic paradox. We are stuck, *deeply*, in the very pit of the paradox. And so, ah sweet relief, we see that we have come upon the end of yet another road. So when someone claims to have revealed truth outside the box of human intellectual experience we are left with truths that can never, ever possibly be proven. And we see a cognitive intellectual limitation, wrapped in the bow of paradox.

The upshot is that talking about the illusoriness of consciousness is about as irrelevant as "deep contemplation" of other universes (no matter how "true" such things might be, we still don't possess a Book of Truth to verify them!). So, WHO CARES! At the end of the day, we're still stuck with *this life* in *this universe* having *this experience*. We do not have outside access to other universes or to a Book of Truth revealing to us all the illusions we have fallen for over the years. Our predicament is so precarious and so undeniably ridiculous that our only recourse is to hope for the best and prepare for the worst. We are forced to resort to a cliché.

Words and words we've rolled through and a picture I've painted, familiar yet new. And now, have you ever heard of the phrase, "the more you understand, seems the less you know?" I think all of thought and reasoning, much like this book, is equivalent to merrily zipping along until arriving at Narrative's End—only to find paradox greeting you on the other side.

We are in a finite position, and we truly do not know our entire relationship with existence and consciousness. It might be insignificant, it might be grandiose. It might even be somewhere in between. The point is that our minds can only take us so far, and then it all falls apart: we meet our old friend paradox. And that's as far as we can go. And so my conclusion is as trite as it is profound; we don't know what's on the other side of the paradox. Is the glass half empty or half full? Through all these words that I've written, our predicament ends up being entirely the same as it's always been! But know that you have every right to believe in meaning and purpose, and know that you have every right to believe in meaninglessness and purposelessness just as well.

I'll leave it as another paradoxical puzzle as to exactly *what* provides legitimacy in my making the above claims! [Hint: we are left at the end of the day with only words and language to console ourselves. Words and language can only take us so far, and then belief constructs take over. And we must be ever aware and skeptical of where our inevitable beliefs might lead us!]

One belief that I am aware of having, and continue to accept, is that our human consciousness is the product of a evolutionary chain of events that has logically and meaningfully varied from a meaningless and pointless necessity (The Self-Writing Script). The result is Pointlessly Meaningful. Like it or not I think this describes Truth in a nutshell. Tying a ribbon on the absurdity, I also believe it's impossible for us to prove any of it, because it's impossible to get beyond our own limiting intelligence (the same intelligence that graciously allowed us to pose the questions in the first place)! And that is my religion.

LAST BYTE:

ALL DONE

http://www.philscanlan.net/

© 2004 by Phil V. Scanlan

The Big and the Small

The young and intellectually-inclined are perhaps more prone to thoughts of the all-encompassing and abstract than are those beaten down by the hard reality of extended years. The young are much more likely to think of worlds within worlds, universes within universes and the like. The young are much more likely to imagine the universe as a sort of organism with its own set of bodily laws from which it is governed. Such thoughts are bold, audacious, and fanciful. The passing of years conditions the young mind to accept a more somber realization of truth—or at least what there might be left of that concept in today's world—that truth is found in the details, in the particulars. A sustainable income is rarely found in all-encompassing and abstract thought. Technical details are difficult to master yet knowledge of the details is critical for anybody concerned about continued employment in most any field. So much for the big stuff.

Interestingly, just as the abstractions of the young can be trite and inarticulate, the particulars of life can be dull when divorced from a more meaning-oriented schema. Our human understanding requires both detail and abstraction for true coherence and meaning. Mechanics and creativity in thought are both needed to achieve true elucidation. Ideally, the combining of the two, the meeting together at the AND/OR, is what our human understanding most craves. This is accomplished through the demonstration of grand theories by way of the minutiae of worldly details.

Every living creature can be looked at as a microcosm—a little universe, shaped by multitudes of tiny self-propagating organisms. Inside this microverse, there are many entities fulfilling the basic requirements of being alive. First, to be alive, an entity must be autopoietic. In other words, it requires the ability to maintain itself against the destructive forces of the outside world. A living entity must constantly adapt to the unforgiving world, while at the same time retaining its own particular identity inside that world. Second, before an entity can be considered living, it must also manage the trick of reproducing itself. Multitudes of tiny entities inside our very bodies meet this criterion. There is in fact a ubiquitous interplay between two levels of reality, with one contextual level having no conscious role in the actions of the other while yet retaining a mutual inter-dependence.

As an example of the deep inter-relationships that exist between the micro and macro worlds, consider the fact that some types of plants (like the pea family) cannot live in nitrogen-deficient soil unless the plants contain nitrogen-fixing bacteria within them. In turn, we humans cannot live without the nitrogen that those bacteria-dependent plants provide. Also consider that neither cows nor termites are capable of digesting the cellulose of grass and wood by themselves. They depend, symbiotically, on communities of microbes inside them to do this digesting. It's even estimated that ten percent of our own dry body weight consists of bacteria. Much of this bacteria is not innate to our bodies, yet our existence depends on them. With such considerations, it's easy to see how the concept of a distinct "individual" can easily be broken down into an ambiguous fuzziness. This rich coexistence gives us a glimpse into a youthful idea of worlds within worlds possessing what can romantically be called an underlying harmony and relatedness of all things. An idea whose context inevitably leads, if looked at linearly enough, to visions of global consciousness. If we step away from the context and allow ourselves to consider the nonlinearities always so prevalent, we can only conclude that we have little comprehension of the world's complexity.

The limitations of our knowledge and reasoning have been examined in this book regarding the possibility of our ever understanding how existence came to exist. Why would our evolutionary survival have led to our possessing esoteric reasoning abilities capable of answering such abstract, otherworldly questions? It was suggested that sweet relief is found in true paradoxes such that when we come across one, we know that we are at the limits of our comprehension. So, what has been accomplished?

Concerning existence, I have provided a framework from which existence can be considered a necessity: the Script. The Script was suggested to be self-writing such that it was forced to "run," a self-contradictory conflict that smacks of utter necessity. Such necessity was shown to be as pointless as it is meaningful, and more significantly to be a mind-numbing paradox. The Script was shown to be a conflict that at its core both followed the "Law" of non-Contradiction and did not follow the "Law" of non-Contradiction.

It was further suggested that to resolve the conflict, the Script was probably forced to "experience" itself, thus Validating its own existence. We then looked at human consciousness, and how it has seemingly evolved over time through natural selection as a patched-together add-on to a more fundamental program.

Comprehensively, the picture I'm presenting is that of a pointlessly meaningful Shiva dance, where everything is relational, everything is linked, and everything is arbitrarily Varying a Theme.

Have I fulfilled my beginning quest? Have I provided a Narrative's End producing an "a-ha" experience?

Honestly, I don't believe the project has completely failed. A new insight has been advanced allowing for the consideration and understanding of a puzzle that has notoriously defied description. That's not chopped liver. But there's certainly room for opinion there. Specifically, the notion of A Variation on a Theme must be weighed as to how much it brings to the table. It casts a Very big net, and admittedly many particulars slip through the holes; we have patched-together add-ons galore. Yet, that might very well capture the type of world we live in; an arbitrary world meaningfully constraining its arbitrariness to a paradoxical Theme. Has the opening puzzle of existence been solved? If the focal-point of our discussion is indeed a paradox, this project merely explains how it can *never* ever be "solved" and that paradoxically, *that's the solution.*

Persuaded?

Now, having sold my wares, what can I expect to be the response? In a nicely satirical little book called *The Dilbert Principle*, author Scott Adams argues for a significant thesis—namely, that people are idiots. Much of his observations center around that fascinating subdivision of human rationality called *irrationality*. He believes that most of what passes for day-to-day "logic" and "breadth of reasoning" can actually be unveiled as self-interest, and unsupportable opinions.

Well, I don't believe that all people are idiots. All of us do, however, have self-interest. After all, we need to make money for shelter, to put food on the table, to buy clothes, to raise our kids, to own a nice car, and to present ourselves as a worthy sex-mate. Once that business is taken care of, other wants and desires have the curious ability of dominating our affairs. It is my sincere contention that humans are multi-faceted. Any one of us can put matters of self-interest to one side (at least temporarily). We can fill our minds **both** with the transpirings of movie stars and sports heroes, **and** still have more than enough room left over to sit back in wide-faced wonder and awe at the twisting, turning, rolling of the Theme. Now that's a Paradox!

At the beginning of this book I mentioned the quixotic nature of my project and the staggering unlikelihood of this meme surviving, let alone thriving. I am not a scientist, I am not a professional philosopher.

A person's passion and obsession is a deep-level emotional, irrational impulse. It's a beginning point, an axiom, that cannot be explained outside of itself. This book's entire rationally-based argument is paradoxically built upon just such an irrational impulse (as must always be the case). Any intellectualist system has its paradoxical limitations. At one and the same time, there is no more important and noble of a goal than to rationally understand the world, but at the end of the day nothing is as important and noble as the nonintellectual act of holding a loved one in your arms. Yes, this is an absurd world we live in. But it can be enjoyable enough.

I believe that this book's meme will thrive in spite of all the obstacles. And I believe it is part of my purpose, a purpose that I have created, to see to it that it does. Make it your own. Pass it on. It's open-source.

I tie this up at the end with the whole paradox thing. Hopefully you've gotten something special from this book—an insight: an understanding that the beginning of things is at the outer edges of our understanding. I hope you have grown to appreciate and welcome paradox. At the end of this book as well as at the beginning of existence—that's all we have.

So What Now?

Biochemist Christian de Duve wrote in *Vital Dust*:

My reasons for seeing the universe as meaningful lie in what I perceive as its built-in necessities. Monod stressed the improbability of life and mind and the preponderant role of chance in their emergence, hence the lack of design in the universe, hence its absurdity and pointlessness. My reading of the same facts is different. It gives chance the same role, but acting within such a stringent set of constraints as to produce life and mind obligatorily, not once but many times. To Monod's famous sentence "the universe was not pregnant with life, nor the biosphere with man," I reply: "You are wrong. They were." (de Duve, 1995)

While I agree with de Duve's analysis that the universe is "pregnant with life," the meaning this may have is not altogether obvious. After all, the pregnancy is brought on by a mindless replaying of a pointless necessity—the conscious-existence, the thing which *cannot not be*. This is the stopping point, the meeting of Being and Non-Being. If you take nothing else from this book, understand this: the world is as meaningful as it is pointless; as rational as it is irrational. It is yet our responsibility to appreciate the good life and to show respect for this curious beast called life.

Perhaps some want more. There remains an emptiness, an incompletion. What even is the "good life" and how, pray tell, does one attain it?

Well, perhaps this question has already been answered many times—although the concepts involved are notoriously difficult to articulate. Perhaps spiritual life is an actual, default process of some sort. Perhaps we, as a particular Variation on a Theme, can be considered inexact copies of that Original Theme (for what else would we be?). This scenario would suggest a built-in relationship, a link, between the Theme and us, the Variation. Now, I'm in no way suggesting that this sort of scenario is at all a logically concise diagram of spiritual life. Consider that a person can as likely be a *mass murderer* as he can be a *living saint*. Both are equally Variations on a Theme, and it could well be argued that in the grand scheme of things being a *living saint* is no more an appropriate Variation of the Theme, then is being a *mass murderer*. Sad, but probably true.

I do not wish to skirt the fact that the world is as full of *ugliness* as it is full of *beauty*, and that we as humans exemplify this as much as anything else (perhaps more so because we are capable of so much more). All the same, there is something that is basic here, that is worth trying to communicate: a certain relationship between man and the universe might be attainable. This is a relationship that has been spoken of since time long lost. The instructions are ancient and universal: Do unto others as you would have others do unto you; love your neighbor as you love yourself; *get rid of* selfishness, pettiness, and idiosyncratic fears and delusions; *strip away* the foolishness of pride; *lose* your illusory sense of "self" and, instead, do without doing, think without thinking, achieve without achieving (as I've mentioned, this is nearly impossible to communicate in any sort of sensible manner); *get rid of yourself* (the fears, the insecurities, and the preconceptions that comprise the sum total of our limitations) and connect whatever remains *without particularly desiring to do so* with the Theme (or Way, or Word, or *li*, etc...). Perhaps we have heard these things many times before. Even so, we no doubt need often to be reminded of

such things: as these are the faint and impenetrable truths that are so easy for us to forget. And what does any of this mean?

In the course of this book, I've presented a very naturalistic, intellectualist program. A program that intrinsically insists that the Theme is a paradox, and that we are ultimately Variations on that Theme. A program that further suggests that the Theme might be conscious of sorts; an "unconscious experiencer." Just consider this for a moment, there's more than one way to view all this. That "unconscious experiencer" can be viewed as a limited, restricted Being that doesn't even possess self-awareness. It can also be viewed as a very simple and elegant life form, possibly eternal, that does not possess our self-conscious weaknesses. Whether it has "knowledge" or is capable of "knowing" us or "loving" us, of course, there would be no way for us to determine. Also, if that life-form does exist, and is eternal, I really don't see how it could possess a complex add-on quality like self-awareness given its contextual basic-ness. Regardless, I just want to stress that the scenario I'm presenting is *open-ended*. There are *things we don't know*, and so belief can legitimately enter into the picture.

Yet, may I suggest something? Something that I alluded to early on in this book? Something to do with paradox? Something to do with accepting it, even reveling in it? The following is from Kent Keith's *Anyway: The Paradoxical Commandments*:

People are illogical, unreasonable, and self-centered.
Love them anyway.

If you do good, people will accuse you of selfish ulterior motives.
Do good anyway.

If you are successful, you will win false friends and true enemies.
Succeed anyway.

The good you do today will be forgotten tomorrow.
Do good anyway.

Honesty and frankness make you vulnerable.
Be honest and frank anyway.

The biggest men and women with the biggest ideas can be shot down by the smallest men and women with the smallest minds.
Think big anyway.

People favor underdogs but follow only top dogs.
Fight for a few underdogs anyway.

What you spend years building may be destroyed overnight.
Build anyway.

People really need help but may attack you if you do help them.
Help people anyway.

Give the world the best you have and you'll get kicked in the teeth.
Give the world the best you have anyway.

Please understand, while I believe that I might have presented a viable Script for existence, most things in this world remain delightfully elusive, and seductively unknown. You see, while ALL might be too big a thing for any of us to entirely understand, the good news is this: we have as much reason to *rejoice* in our predicament as we do to *lament*. By this I mean that, by default, we have a *choice*: the world is not entirely *this way* or *that way*, but is instead *a little bit of both*.

And now I close with analogy, with poetry:

That is It : It is That
Are we as much products of *fate* as *creators of fate*? Are we as compelled by hallucinations as by rational thought? Are we as much an outcome of Chance as of Design?

Sadly, joyously! It's that Knot, that Paradox, that Thing Which *Cannot Not Be*. *It's self-aware…It Knows.* How beautiful—for it couldn't be any other way. And yet, and yet, how horrible, how terrible—is that all there is? At the heart of All Things…is that it? Yet it couldn't be any other way. Here we are—face to face *with what?* A Knot, a Tangle, a Paradox? Could that really be?

And that is why it came to be.
And that is why the world is here.
And that is why it was no mistake.
It had to all be just this way.
It's love, it's hate, it's life, it's death.

And I don't know what more to say.
To live, to breathe, to laugh, to cry.
These things we have, is that all there is?
Is this all there is to be alive?
To joke, to abuse, to punish, to care.
These things we have, are all we have.
This life, I love—I love myself.
But then again, I was born that way.
Sometimes, even, I think the same about God.
These words—they should be said in a whisper.
Because they really should never, ever be spoken.
And that is it, it is that.

Do we revolt? Scoff? Murder? Destroy? Anything goes, right? It's all a meaningless Knot. And yet, and yet, *that is it*. That's why there's Anything At All, that's why there's self-awareness, that's the way it had to be—for better or worse. Is not that Knot sentient? Is not that Knot Divine and Holy? Is not that Knot as much a subject for explicable enquiry as a subject for awe and wonder? Should not that Knot be worshipped and glorified?

Do we respond with hate and venom—*how dare that be all there is, how appalling!* Do we respond with empathy and understanding? That Knot, that Wonderful Knot, is the Source of ALL THINGS!

Does it get "lonely"? Is it "proud" of us?

The mystery solved! What now? Do we shed a *tear of joy*? Do we shed of *tear of sorrow*? Or maybe, possibly, could it really be…why? why? *why* did it have to be this way?

Both.

The Theme (to the tune of Edgar Allan Poe's *The Bells*)

Ah!—
The Theme,—
What a Theme!
What a Very, Very, Vary—
What a Theme!
What a Constant Way of Slipping for this Game that Keeps a-Drifting
In this—the Twisting, Turning, Rolling of the Theme
What a Theme!
This Great Sprawling Mess is a Very, Very, Vary—
Endlessly…, Endlessly…, Pulsing…, Pounding…
What a Theme!
What a Very, Very, Vary—
What a Theme!
Ah,—
The Theme,—
What a Theme!
It was curled up—like in a Ring
Ready, to Spring!
Now—Rolling, Rolling, Rolling
It cannot help but keep a-Rolling
All Glory is in this Rolling of the Theme
What a Theme!
What a Very, Very, Vary—
What a Theme!
That Theme, Theme, Theme
Is it all but a Dream?
As it Pounds, Pounds, Pounds, Pounds,
Pounds,
What A Very Fine Theme!
What a Theme!
And its Merry Music Swells…
    It's the Slipping and the Drifting of the—
    Twisting and the Turning of the—
    Pulsing and the Pounding of the—
    Throbbing and the Swelling of the—
    Another Variation of the—

Very, Very, Vary,
Keeping Time, Time, Time,
As it Folds, Folds, Folds,
in the Pulsing, Pounding, Rolling of the—
        Twisting, Turning, Folding of the—
Ah!—
The Theme!
What a Theme!
What a-, What a-, What a-, What a-, What a-,
What a Very Fine Theme!

REFERENCES

http://science.howstuffworks.com/brain.htm
http://www.deakin.edu.au/hbs/GAGEPAGE/

Aunger, Robert, *The Electric Meme: A New Theory of How We Think*, The Free Press, New York, 2002.

Bagemihl, Bruce, *Biological Exuberance: Animal Homosexuality and Natural Diversity*, St. Martin's Press, New York, 1999.

Balkin, J.M., *Cultural Software: A Theory of Ideology*, Yale University Press, New Haven, 1998.

Bandler, Richard, & Grinder, John, *The Structure of Magic*, Science and Behavior Books, Inc., Palo Alto, CA, 1975.

Barabasi, Albert-Laszlo, *Linked: The New Science of Networks*, Perseus Publishing, Cambridge, Massachusetts, 2002.

Barash, David P., *Sociobiology and Behavior*, Elsevier, New York, 1977.

Barrow, John D., *The Book of Nothing*, Pantheon Books, New York, 2000.

_____, *Impossibility: The Limits of Science and the Science of Limits*, Oxford University Press, Oxford, 1998.

_____, & Frank J. Tipler, *The Anthropic Cosmological Principle*, Oxford University Press, Oxford, 1996.

_____, *The Constants of Nature*, Pantheon Books, New York, 2002.

Beeler, Nelson F. & Branley, Franklyn M., *Experiments in Optical Illusion*, Thomas Y. Crowell Company, New York, 1951.

Blackmore, Susan, *Dying to Live: Near-Death Experiences*, Prometheus Books, 1993.

_____, *The Meme Machine*, Oxford University Press, New York, 1999.

_____, *Beyond the Body*, Academy Chicago Publishers, Chicago, 1982.

_____, *In Search of the Light*, Prometheus Books, Amherst, New York, 1996.

Bloom Howard, *Global Brain*, John Wiley & Sons, Inc., New York, 2000.

Bohm, David, *Wholeness and the Implicate Order*, Routledge, London and New York, 1995.

Brown, Julian, *Minds, Machines, and the Multiverse: The Quest for the Quantum Computer*, Simon & Schuster, New York, 2000.

Buchanan, Mark, *Ubiquity*, Crown Publishers, New York, 2000.

Buss, David M., *The Evolution of Desire*, BasicBooks, New York, 1994.

Camp, L. Sprague de, *The Ancient Engineers*, Barnes & Noble Books, New York, 1993.

Carter, Rita, *Mapping the Mind*, University of California Press, Berkeley, 1998.

Cheney, Dorothy L. & Seyfarth, Robert M., *How Monkeys See the World*, University of Chicago Press, Chicago, 1990.

Cherfas, Jeremy & Gribbin, John, *The Redundant Male*, Pantheon Books, New York, 1984.

Cialdini, Robert B, *Influence: The Psychology of Persuasion*, Quill William Morrow, New York, 1993.

Close, Frank, *Lucifer's Legacy: the Meaning of Asymmetry*, Oxford University Press, New York, 2000.

Cohen, Jack & Steward, Ian, *The Collapse of Chaos*, Penguin Books, New York, 1994.

Cremo, Michael A. & Thompson, Richard L., *Forbidden Archeology*, Bhaktivedanta Book Publishing, Inc., Los Angeles, 1996.

_____, *The Hidden History of the Human Race*, Govardhan Hill Publishing, Badger, California, 1994.

Damasio, Antonio, *The Feeling of What Happens: Body and Emotion in the Making of Consciousness*, A Harvest Book, San Diego, 1999.

_____, *Descartes" Error*, An Avon Book, New York, 1994.

Davies, Paul, *The Fifth Miracle: The Search for the Origin and Meaning of Life*, Simon & Schuster, New York, 1999.

Davis, Martin, *Computability and Unsolvability*, Dover Publications, Inc., New York, 1982.

Dawkins, Richard, *The Selfish Gene*, Oxford University Press, reissued 1989.

_____, *Unweaving the Rainbow*, Mariner Books, Boston, 1998.

de Bono, Edward, *de Bono's Thinking Course*, FactsOnFile, New York, 1994.

de Mello, Anthony, One Minute Wisdom, Doubleday & Company, Inc., Garden City, New York, 1986.

Dennett, Daniel C., *Consciousness Explained*, BackBay Books, Boston, 1991.

_____, *Darwin's Dangerous Idea*, Simon & Schuster, New York, 1996.

Deutsch, David, *The Fabric of Reality*, Allen Lane—The Penguin Press, New York, 1997.

Dyson, George, *Darwin Among the Machines*, Allen Lane—The Penguin Press, New York, 1997.

Edelman, Gerald, Bright Air, Brilliant Fire, BasicBooks, New York, 1992.

Emrich, Duncan, *The Nonsense Book*, Four Winds Press, New York, 1970.

Ferris, Timothy, *Coming of Age in the Milky Way*, Anchor Books, New York, 1988.

Freeman, Derek, *Margaret Mead and Samoa*, Harvard University Press, Cambridge, MA, 1983.

Gardner, Howard, *Frames of Mind: The Theory of Multiple Intelligences*, Basic Books, Inc., Publishers, New York, 1983.

Gardner, Martin, *The Colossal Book of Mathematics*, W.W. Norton & Company, New York, 2001.

Gladwell, Malcolm, *The Tipping Point: How Little Things Can Make a Big Difference*, Little, Brown, and Company, New York, 2000.

Goodwin, Brian, *How the Leopard Changed Its Spots: The Evolution of Complexity*, Charles Scribner's Sons, New York, 1994.

Gould, Stephen Jay, *The Structure of Evolutionary Theory*, The Belknap Press of Harvard University Press, Cambridge, Massachusetts, 2002.

_____, *Ever Since Darwin*, W.W. Norton & Company, New York, 1977.

Greenfield, Susan, *The Private Life of the Brain*, John Wiley & Sons, Inc., New York, 2000.

_____, *The Human Brain: A Guided Tour*, Basic Books, New York, 1997.

Gregory, Richard L., *The Oxford Companion to the Mind*, Oxford University Press, 1987.

Harris, Judith Rich, *The Nurture Assumption*, The Free Press, New York, 1998.

Harris, Marvin, *Cows, Pigs, Wars, and Witches: The Riddles of Culture*, Random House, New York, 1974.

Hawking, Stephen, *The Universe in a Nutshell*, Bantam Books, New York, 2001.

Hoffman, Donald, *Visual Intelligence*, W.W. Norton & Company, New York, 1998.

Holland, John H., *Hidden Order: How Adaptation Builds Complexity*, Helix Books, Reading, Massachusetts, 1995.

Horgan, John, *The Undiscovered Mind: How the Human Brain Defies Replication, Medication, and Explanation*, A Touchstone Book, New York, 1999.

Jaynes, Julian, *The Origin of Consciousness in the Breakdown of the Bicameral Mind*, Houghton Mifflin Company, Boston, 1976.

Johnson, Steven, *Emergence: The Connected Lives of Ants, Brains, Cities, and Software*, Scribner, New York, 2001.

Kaplan, Robert D. *Warrior Politics: Why Leadership Demands a Pagan Ethos*, Random House, New York, 2002.

Katz, Steven T. (ed.), *Mysticism and Language*, Oxford University Press, New York, 1992.

Kelly, Kevin, *Out of Control: The New Biology of Machines, Social Systems, and the Economic World*, Addison-Wesley Publishing Company, Reading, Massachusetts, 1994.

Keith, Kent M., *Anyway: The Paradoxical Commandments*, G.P. Putnam's Sons, New York, 2001.

Kosko, Bart, *Fuzzy Thinking*, Hyperion, New York, 1993.

Lamarck, J.B., Elliot, Hugh (trans.), *Zoological Philosophy*, The University of Chicago Press, Chicago, 1984.

LeDoux, Joseph, *Synaptic Self*, Viking, New York, 2002.

Lewontin, R. C., Rose, Steven, & Kamin, Leon J., *Not In Our Genes: Biology, Ideology, and Human Nature*, Pantheon Books, New York, 1984.

Ludwig, Arnold M., *The Price of Greatness*, The Guilford Press, New York, 1995.

Margulis, Lynn & Sagan, Dorion, *Microcosmos: Four Billion Years of Evolution from Our Microbial Ancestors*, Summit Books, New York, 1986.

_____, *Mystery Dance: On the Evolution of Human Sexuality*, Summit Books, New York, 1991.

_____, *Symbiotic Planet: A New View of Evolution*, BasicBooks, New York, 1998.

Mayr, Ernst, *What Evolution Is*, BasicBooks, New York, 2001.

Mcginn, Colin, *The Mysterious Flame: Conscious Minds in a Material World*, Basic Books, New York, 1999.

Ninio, Jacques (trans. By Franklin Philip), *The Science of Illusions*, Cornell University Press, Ithica & London, 1998.

Nolte, David D., *Mind at Light Speed: A New Kind of Intelligence*, The Free Press, New York, 2001.

Odenwald, Sten, *The Astronomy Café*, W. H. Freeman and Company, New York, 1998.

_____, *Patterns In The Void: Why Nothing Is Important*, WestView Press, 2002.

Parkinson, G.H.R. (ed.), Morris, Mary & Parkinson, G.H.R. (trans.), *Leibniz Philosophical Writings*, JM Dent & Sons Ltd, London, 1973.

Peat, F. David, *The Philosopher's Stone*, Bantam Books, New York, 1991.

_____, *Synchronicity: The Bridge Between Matter and Mind*, Bantam Books, New York, 1987.

Piattelli-Palmarini, Massimo, *Inevitable Illusions: How Mistakes of Reason Rule our Minds*, John Wiley & Sons, Inc., New York, 1994.

Pickover, Clifford A., *The Loom of God: Mathematical Tapestries at the Edge of Time*, Plenum Trade, New York, 1997.

_____, *Synchronicity: The Bridge Between Matter and Mind*, Bantam Books, New York, 1987.

_____, The Paradox of God: And the Science of Omniscience, Palgrave, New York, 2001.

_____, *Strange Brains and Genius*, Plenum Trade, New York, 1998.

_____, *The Girl Who Gave Birth to Rabbits*, Prometheus Books, Amherst, New York, 2000.

_____, *dreaming the future*, Prometheus Books, Amherst, New York, 2001.

Pinker, Steven, *The Language Instinct*, HarperPerennial, New York, 1994.

_____, *How the Mind Works*, W.W. Norton & Co., New York, 1997.

_____, *Words and Rules*, BasicBooks, New York, 1999.

_____, *The Blank Slate: The Modern Denial of Human Nature*, Viking, New York, 2002.

Poundstone, William, *The Recursive Universe*, Contemporary Books, Inc., Chicago, 1985.

Price, Richard (Intro), *The Future of Spacetime*, W. W. Norton & Company, New York, 2002.

Quinn, Daniel, *Beyond Civilization: Humanity's Next Great Adventure*, Harmony Books, New York, 1999.

Ramachandran, V.S, & Sandra Blakeslee, *Phantoms in the Brain*, William Morrow and Company, Inc., New York, 1998.

Randi, James, *Flim Flam!*, Prometheus Books, Buffalo, New York, 1982

Ratey, John J., *A User's Guide to the Brain*, Pantheon Books, New York, 2001.

Rees, Martin, *Out Cosmic Habitat*, Princeton University Press, 2001.

Ring, Kenneth, *The Omega Project*, William Morrow and Company, Inc., New York, 1992.

Ryle, Gilbert, *The Concept of Mind*, The University of Chicago Press, 1949.

Sabom, Michael, *Light & Death*, Zondervan Publishing House, Grand Rapids, Michigan, 1998.

Sheldradke, Rupert, *The Presence of the Past*, Park Street Press, Rochester, Vermont, 1995.

Shermer, Michael, *The Borderlands of Science*, Oxford University Press, New York 2001.

_____, *Why People Believe Weird Things*, Henry Holt and Company, New York, 2002.

Sitchin, Zecharia, *The 12th Planet*, Avon Books, New York, 1976.

_____, *The Wars of Gods and Men*, Avon Books, New York, 1985.

Smullyan, Raymond M., *The Tao is Silent*, HarperSanFrancisco, 1977.

_____, *Satan, Cantor, and Infinity*, Alfred A. Knopf, New York, 1992.

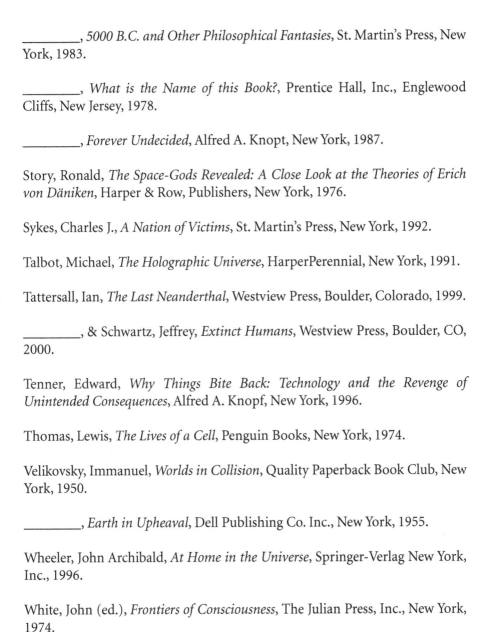
_____, *5000 B.C. and Other Philosophical Fantasies*, St. Martin's Press, New York, 1983.

_____, *What is the Name of this Book?*, Prentice Hall, Inc., Englewood Cliffs, New Jersey, 1978.

_____, *Forever Undecided*, Alfred A. Knopt, New York, 1987.

Story, Ronald, *The Space-Gods Revealed: A Close Look at the Theories of Erich von Däniken*, Harper & Row, Publishers, New York, 1976.

Sykes, Charles J., *A Nation of Victims*, St. Martin's Press, New York, 1992.

Talbot, Michael, *The Holographic Universe*, HarperPerennial, New York, 1991.

Tattersall, Ian, *The Last Neanderthal*, Westview Press, Boulder, Colorado, 1999.

_____, & Schwartz, Jeffrey, *Extinct Humans*, Westview Press, Boulder, CO, 2000.

Tenner, Edward, *Why Things Bite Back: Technology and the Revenge of Unintended Consequences*, Alfred A. Knopf, New York, 1996.

Thomas, Lewis, *The Lives of a Cell*, Penguin Books, New York, 1974.

Velikovsky, Immanuel, *Worlds in Collision*, Quality Paperback Book Club, New York, 1950.

_____, *Earth in Upheaval*, Dell Publishing Co. Inc., New York, 1955.

Wheeler, John Archibald, *At Home in the Universe*, Springer-Verlag New York, Inc., 1996.

White, John (ed.), *Frontiers of Consciousness*, The Julian Press, Inc., New York, 1974.

Wilson, Edward O., *The Insect Societies*, The Belknap Press of Harvard University Press, Cambridge, Massachusetts, 1971.

Wolfram, Stephen, *A New Kind of Science*, Wolfram Media, Inc., Champaign, IL, 2002.

Wright, Robert, *The Moral Animal*, Vintage Books, New York, 1994.

INDEX

D

E

F

G

H

I

0-595-31777-4

www.ingramcontent.com/pod-product-compliance
Lightning Source LLC
Chambersburg PA
CBHW051233050326
40689CB00007B/908